# WHY PHILANTHROPY MATTERS

# WHY
# PHILANTHROPY
# MATTERS

How the Wealthy Give, and What It
Means for Our Economic Well-Being

## ZOLTAN J. ACS

PRINCETON UNIVERSITY PRESS
PRINCETON AND OXFORD

Ács, Zoltán J.
Why philanthropy matters : how the wealthy give, and what it means for our economic
 well-being / Zoltan J. Acs.
 p. cm.
Includes bibliographical references and index.
ISBN 978-0-691-14862-5 (hbk. : alk. paper) 1. Endowments. 2. Rich people—Charitable
 contributions. 3. Humanitarianism—Economic aspects. 4. Entrepreneurship—Social
 aspects. 5. Capitalism—Social aspects. I. Title.
HV25.A27 2013
361.7'4—dc23       2012031852

British Library Cataloging-in-Publication Data is available

This book has been composed in Sabon

Printed on acid-free paper. ∞

Printed in the United States of America

10 9 8 7 6 5 4 3 2 1

*Dedicated to Ashley and Annabel*

# CONTENTS

# PREFACE

It is often said that discoveries large and small are historical accidents. The discovery of America is one of those accidents. Christopher Columbus was looking for a sea route to India and discovered the Americas. The story of this book is no exception. In 1976, I was a graduate student trying to understand the American economy from the perspective of large corporations and large unions for my dissertation. In particular, I was looking at the U.S. steel industry, but it could have been any one of several large managed industries in America at the time. While trying to understand inflation, I discovered a peculiar anomaly about American-style capitalism.

While large steel firms like United States Steel were having a difficult time competing in the global marketplace, entrepreneurs were starting new steel companies all over America and competing with the big boys and the Japanese. Of course this would not have been an interesting story but for the fact that large firms were supposed to be technologically and organizationally superior to any small firm in the economy. Thus I began an interesting journey to explain how the United States was evolving from a managerial economy to an entrepreneurial society.

Over the decades following this accidental discovery I became a student of entrepreneurship and innovation: big business and small business, low technology and high technology, America and the rest of the world. My partner in much of this was David B. Audretsch, whom I met in 1979. With a suitcase full of data we traveled to Berlin together, trying to decipher the secrets of large and small firms, of innovation, and of technological change. I am deeply indebted to him for the years of collaboration and thoughtful scholarship.

In Berlin at the WZB (an island behind the Iron Curtain), David and I unraveled some of the secrets of how entrepreneurs were transforming the U.S. economy and how government was systematically dismantling the managerial economy. Over the decades, we established an understanding of how the small-firm sector operated and why it was important for the economy.

In 1989, I moved back to the United States and took a position at the University of Baltimore. These were exciting times. The entrepreneurial revolution was under way and the United States was in the driver's seat. The Berlin Wall had just fallen, communism was relegated to the dustbin of history, and the future looked bright. Entrepreneurs were starting to transform the world. The information revolution was in full swing.

It was at this time that I met Richard Florida and we started to collaborate on the importance of innovation and cities. This was a hot topic, as Boston's Route 128 and Silicon Valley were the sources of the information revolution and understanding how these two regions spawned this revolution was on everyone's mind. As countries shed central planning and state ownership, the world was looking for a market solution to its problems. Richard and I, along with Maryann Feldman, Attila Varga, and Sam Yung Lee, started to better understand the importance of cities and entrepreneurship in economic development. Richard has continued to be a valuable colleague over the years.

During the mid-1990s I spent five years in Washington, DC. My first appointment was at the U.S. Small Business Administration. I was no stranger to the agency, having used its data in much of my previous research. While at the SBA I recognized the need to develop policies to support an entrepreneurial economy. The policy agenda of the managerial economy was well worked out, but the details of how an entrepreneurial economy functions and can be supported were less well known. In Washington, I met Catherine Armington, with whom I worked for several years at the U.S. Bureau of the Census. I am grateful for her support.

The second part of the historical accident happened when my longtime friend Andrew Capitman, an investment banker, suggested to me that American-style capitalism was as much about philanthropy as about entrepreneurship. He said, "Look at all these beautiful buildings at Yale University; they were all donated by some rich guy." The challenge was to figure out how these two pieces of the puzzle fit together. How did philanthropy fit into American-style capitalism? It sounded like Taoist philosophy: light and dark, yin and yang. Everything has both yin and yang aspects as light cannot exist without darkness, and vice versa, but either of these aspects may manifest more strongly in particular objects, and may ebb or flow over time.

I was intrigued, so I did what any good scholar would do: I looked for books on entrepreneurship and philanthropy. Because this was an interesting subject, I was sure that it had been well researched by scholars. Having a good handle on the entrepreneurship literature, I started to read about philanthropy. I discovered a large literature on everything from wealthy individuals to great foundations, but I could not find anything written that tied these two topics together. The more I looked the more intrigued I became, not with what I had discovered but with what I could not find.

I met up with an old friend and colleague at the American Economic Association meetings, where I had just presented a paper on the subject to an unsympathetic audience. Ronnie Phillips, a professor at Northern Colorado University, was a student of American institutionalism, so I explained to him what puzzled me. He was interested and we started a research project on entrepreneurship and philanthropy. After three long years, we had a rudimentary understanding of what we were searching for. The story was sketchy at best and incomplete but it started to make sense. America was different, and it had forgotten that it was.

Following this, Pontus Braunerhjelm at the Royal Academy in Sweden and I started to work on the subject. We carried out several projects on entrepreneurship and philanthropy comparing Sweden and Ohio. Putting this into the context of economic growth, we started to explain why the United States outperformed Europe. At the same time, Leo Paul Dana at McGill University and I worked on philanthropy in China.

In 2004, David Audretsch and I went back to Germany and set up a research unit on entrepreneurship, growth, and public policy at the Max Planck Institute of Economics in Jena. The world was trying to figure out how an entrepreneurial economy functioned in America, in Europe, and in the rest of the world. I was convinced that philanthropy had to be part of the story. The institute became the leading research center trying to understand entrepreneurship in the twenty-first century and provided fertile ground for sorting out some of these ideas.

In 2005, I moved to George Mason University. The School of Public Policy (SPP) at George Mason University really opened a window on my research. Here I became familiar with the subject of American exceptionalism. Roger Stough, the associate dean of the SPP, was intrigued by the idea and I appreciate his support. I started to work with a group of highly talented graduate students at the SPP: Hezekiah Agwara, Mary Boardman, Pamela Callahan, Sammie Desai, Michelle McAddo, David Miller, Joseph Sany, Nicola Virgil, and Vekataramana (Rama) Yananaudra. Mary and Rama provided valuable research assistance on understanding entrepreneurs and philanthropists through the centuries.

I also accepted an appointment as a senior scholar at the Ewing Marion Kauffman Foundation in Kansas City, where I met Carl Schramm, the foundation's president. He was the first person I met who understood that my discovery was important and who had a very similar view on the importance of philanthropy and entrepreneurship in American-style capitalism. His insights were invaluable.

In 2009, I took a sabbatical at the Imperial College Business School in London. This gave me a chance to think in a systematic way about how philanthropy fit into capitalism. My colleagues Erkko Autio and David Gann provided an ideal working environment; I thank them deeply for this opportunity. By the end of the summer I had a draft of the manuscript. It appeared that there was an untold story here, and I started to piece it together.

In the fall of 2009, Mary Boardman and I spent the semester researching charity and philanthropy in the United Kingdom and the United States. This proved to be immensely helpful to the story. My longtime collaborator and colleague Philip Auerswald asked me to coauthor an article on prosperity. Some of the ideas began fitting together into a story about American-style capitalism.

An event in the summer of 2010 transformed my research, as scores of billionaires in the United States signed a pledge to give away their money. In the fall semester of 2010, Michelle McAddo, a graduate student in economics at George Mason University, helped me weave the story together in a way that would be more understandable to a wider audience. Her help was invaluable. My team expanded as Pamela Callahan started to do research on the Giving Pledge and David Miller pulled together the history of American colleges, entrepreneurship, and the closing of the American frontier for his dissertation.

I returned to Imperial College in the summer of 2011 and wrote a second draft of the book. I now had what I thought was a good story about entrepreneurship and philanthropy. I would like to thank Dody Riggs, who went through several drafts of the manuscript with great care, and Madeleine B. Adams, who edited the final manuscript and provided developmental assistance.

Special thanks to Peter Dougherty at Princeton University Press, who immediately understood what the book was about and steered it in a more focused direction—the underappreciated role of philanthropy in American-style capitalism. Bringing the manuscript back to this central focus necessitated a more detailed account of American history, American politics, and opportunity creation.

I am happy to thank Ashley Acs at Princeton University, who placed the extraordinary depth and breadth of his scholarship on American politics at my disposal, patiently read many drafts of the manuscript, guided me away from misstatements and misunderstandings, and provided me with invaluable research assistance in pulling the final version of the manuscript together. He carried out research on several of the chapters, helped reorganize the manuscript, and brought his immense knowledge of the craft of writing to bear on the subject. Although Ashley is as yet a graduate student and I am long a professor, in this undertaking the roles were often reversed, to my great benefit.

In addition to those mentioned earlier, I would like to thank Alan J. Abramson, Bo Carlsson, Leo Paul Dana, Jack Goldstone, David Hart, Kingsley Haynes, Jill Kickul, Szerb Laszlo, Connie McNeally, Jay Mitra, John Munkirs, Larry Plummer, Edward Rhodes, Mark Sanders, Siri Terjesen, Roy Thurik, Attila Varga, Thomas Vietorisz, Robert Wuebker, and colleagues at George Mason University and Imperial College London for valuable comments and discussions. Imre Kovacs, Kevin McCarthy, Oliver Rothschild, Spencer Stacy, and Tom Vander Ark all freely gave time and suggestions.

A special thanks to my wife, Jane, and my family, who had to put up with fifteen years of discussions about entrepreneurship and philanthropy.

# WHY PHILANTHROPY MATTERS

# CHAPTER 1

# A CONVERSATION

He who dies rich dies in disgrace.
—ANDREW CARNEGIE

## The Giving Pledge

On August 3, 2010, the *Wall Street Journal* ran an article titled "U.S. Super Rich to Share Wealth."[1] The piece was about the Giving Pledge—an effort by Bill Gates and Warren Buffett to get the world's richest individuals and families to give away half of their wealth during their lifetimes. The pledge's initial outreach effort, which stemmed from Gates and Buffett's conversations with wealthy individuals over the previous year, ended with forty American billionaires signing on. The article, published a day after the signing, was buried inside the paper and initially didn't seem to create much excitement.

I expected the story to die, like the patchwork of other newspaper and magazine articles on philanthropy that I had been following over the previous decade—but the Giving Pledge story had legs! Within three months of the signing, it was one of the most talked-about topics in the country, and by the end of the year 7 percent of the traffic on Twitter concerned it. The Giving Pledge has shaken public discourse on the topic of philanthropy and reopened a debate on the role that philanthropy plays in American capitalism.

Reading the letters of many of the signatories sheds light on what these philanthropists hoped to accomplish by giving their money away. George Lucas, the creator of the *Star Wars* franchise, wrote on the Giving Pledge website that he was "dedicating the majority of my wealth to improving education. It is the key to the survival of the human race."[2] Paul Allen of Microsoft wrote, "We will look for new opportunities to make a difference in the lives of future generations."[3] Pierre Omidyar, the founder of eBay, wrote, "People are inherently capable but frequently lack opportunity. . . . . Our common challenge is . . . . leaving a legacy of hope for those to come."[4]

Many of the letters written by the signatories of the Giving Pledge equate philanthropic giving with the creation of new opportunities for individuals. As I hope to show in this book, this cycle of giving—from philanthropy to new opportunity creation—has been an essential ingredient of American capitalism throughout the country's history. Americans' motivations for giving money, as well as the outputs of their generosity, are woven into the entrepreneurial spirit of America—a system that has both nurtured private innovation and sustained a pattern of private giving that exceeds three hundred billion dollars every year.

Despite the apparent generosity of signatories like George Lucas and Paul Allen, much of the public response to the Giving Pledge has been critical, often laced with cynicism about the motives of philanthropy and the extent to which philanthropy undercuts democratic processes. The *Weekly Standard*'s readers attacked the Giving Pledge as "grandstanding," a "publicity stunt," or "the work of socialists."

The German magazine *Der Spiegel* reported in its international edition, "One billionaire 'blasted the effort as a bad transfer of power from the state to billionaires.' "[5] These attacks are misguided, however, because they fail to appreciate that philanthropy, far from being a new fad, is endemic to the entrepreneurial system from which it originated.

In addition to those who criticize philanthropy for its lack of accountability, others question what philanthropic giving can hope to accomplish. Carlos Slim, a Mexican telecommunications magnate who in 2010 overtook Bill Gates as the world's richest man, scoffed at the Giving Pledge, saying, "Charity doesn't solve anything."[6] Slim, himself a philanthropist, questioned whether contributions promised by signatories of the Giving Pledge would result in any measurable improvement for society. His provocative statement raises an interesting question, although perhaps not the one he intended. How do we define, or categorize, philanthropy vis-à-vis charity? As I will maintain throughout this book, it is important to think of philanthropy and charity as two separate things, even though they are often equated in public discourse and in reactions to events like the Giving Pledge.

Philanthropy necessitates a reciprocal relationship between the philanthropist and the beneficiary. When a philanthropist makes an investment, it requires the recipient to make some investment—such as in time and energy—to benefit from the largesse. For example, consider the case of a wealthy individual who donates money to start a university, as Leland Stanford did when founding the university that bears his dead son's name. The recipients of Leland Stanford's largesse—namely, students—do not benefit without making their own investment of the time and energy necessary to earn a degree from Stanford University. In short, philanthropy is an investment that stimulates other investments. Charity, by contrast, requires no such reciprocal relationship. Soup kitchens are charitable, for example, because the recipient need only show up to receive the benefit.

So what? you may ask. Isn't the distinction minor? Haven't we always had both charity and philanthropy? The simple answer is yes. We have always had charity. Alms giving is as old as civilization. We have also had some form of philanthropy for a very long time. Patronage of the arts is also as old as civilization. What is new is America's invented use of philanthropy as a vehicle not for its own ends but for the creation of opportunity for the broad middle class, to build a better society in the long run through hard work and sacrifice. The mix of charity and philanthropy matters. I do not want to argue that charity is bad, just that only charitable gifts that result in the creation of economic and social opportunity for individuals qualify as philanthropy. Philanthropy has a positive long-term externality for society, that is, it creates a better society in the long run.

Philanthropy touches aspects of American society from early childhood education programs to cutting-edge research on biotechnology. When one considers where the preponderance of money that is given away actually goes, the reciprocal relationship inherent in philanthropy begins to make more sense. Consider the biotech industry, in which the contributions made by philanthropists bear fruit only if they are met with trained scientists who can turn research dollars into life-saving medicines. The opportunity afforded to those in research is a reciprocal relationship, as is the ability of life-saving medicines to allow people to rejoin the workforce.

## Philanthropy and America

The Giving Pledge is certainly one of the highest-profile discussions of philanthropy in recent history, and it singles out the commitment that some American business leaders have to extending opportunity beyond what is provided by the marketplace. But how much do the actions of those individuals reflect a broader, more ingrained feature of American generosity and giving? In this book, I argue that to understand philanthropy is to understand something about the American psyche and its fidelity to promoting enterprise and opportunity.

The Giving Pledge has reignited an American conversation about philanthropy, but this new conversation has roots in an ongoing dialogue that can be traced back to those who first left England. Consider, for example, a sermon that the Puritan leader John Winthrop delivered in 1630 on board the ship *Arabella* as it sailed to the New World. Winthrop's shipmates in part were seeking refuge from religious intolerance. Appropriately, Winthrop's sermon was titled "A Model of Christian Charity," yet it laid forth a number of practical ideas about the necessity of industry and hard work, on the one hand, and the importance of frugality and humility, on the other.

These early colonists who came from England in the seventeenth and eighteenth centuries left a society that was on the cusp of experiencing an enormous burst of entrepreneurial activity, invention, and economic growth. But it was also a closed society, where the ability to participate was largely limited to those with land and title. This was most apparent in the landed aristocracy with their vast wealth and disproportionate political influence. Yet even the great advances that would fuel the wool and textile industry in England benefited almost exclusively those with inherited lands who used this wealth to purchase inclusion in this period of entrepreneurial upheaval.

If the Puritans were around today, they might not be wholly pleased with the state of affairs in American business. The Puritans were wary of excessive profit making, reflecting their distaste, not for enterprise and industry, but rather for windfall profits divorced from self-reliance and hard work. Similarly, today the American psyche seems torn between its love affair with entrepreneurial success and its uneasiness with the trappings of inherited wealth. Thus, long before Andrew Carnegie proclaimed his so-called Gospel of Wealth, the Puritans and other early American colonists leaving Europe were laying an intellectual and moral foundation on which successive generations of enterprising Americans would build, helping to ensure that entrepreneurial profit seeking in the New World bore little resemblance to the entitled rent seeking of the Old World.[7] Rent-seeking behavior is an attempt by an interested party (in this case the nobility) to alter the rewards in society in their own favor. This type of behavior does not increase wealth in society; it just changes its distribution.

Through these values, the American experiment has triumphed on a balance between altruistic behavior and self-interest. Self-interest and altruism, though very different motives for human activity, are in fact fundamental traits of human nature and both are crucial to maintaining the strength and vitality of any society. Philanthropy, as I argue in this book, is part of the implicit social contract that continuously nurtures and revitalizes a society.

Philanthropy is also an invisible, underappreciated force for progress in American-style capitalism—the secret ingredient that fails to get mentioned in economic accounts of capitalism. Including it gives us a fuller, more realistic picture of capitalism, and therefore a better handle on how to govern it. We have to rethink the economics of capitalism to incorporate the role of philanthropy—just as we did for entrepreneurship, following Joseph Schumpeter—if we are to create policies to promote its better aspects.[8]

## American-Style Capitalism

In the aftermath of the Great Recession, the future of capitalism in America has moved to the forefront of debate in the United States. One strain of this new conversation has questioned whether the United States ought to move in the direction of Europe, toward a more robust government involvement in the marketplace. In many ways, this knee-jerk reaction to a financial crisis that was fueled by greed and inadequate oversight, and followed by a sustained period of economic malaise, is typical. The standard paradigm observers of capitalism use to understand the American system focuses on conflict between big and small government—privatized health care versus government-run programs, unions versus business, and regulation versus individual freedom.[9]

These old debates—which harken back to the ideological conflicts over the New Deal and the Great Society, as well as to American disagreements over the merits of European-style social democracy—undercut our focus on the entrepreneurial ingredients of American capitalism. Innovation in America will not live or die based on whether we build one more government agency, or how we decide the particulars of labor disputes between large corporations and unions. What is of consequence, however, is how policymakers work to create the conditions necessary to incubate innovation and to nurture an environment in which these innovations can be efficiently commercialized.

Capitalism requires an interplay between individuals and government—between commerce and control. On this point, even the most extreme right-wing and left-wing political factions generally agree. Each society chooses its own rules to govern this interplay. What is American-style capitalism and is it distinct from other styles? American-style capitalism has pushed against the protected relationships between business and government that typify what I consider the worst examples of capitalism throughout the world.[10] There are, of course, many differences between the United States and Europe. Europe has different labor markets and labor laws, and its social services (such as universal health care) are much stronger.[11] But one crucial difference is the degree of entrepreneurial activity and innovation. Europe gave birth to just twelve new big companies between 1950 and 2007. America produced fifty-two in the same period. And Europe has only three firms founded between 1975 and 2007 on a list of the world's five hundred largest publicly traded companies.[12]

I have spent my academic career studying entrepreneurship, predominately in the United States and Europe, but also globally. I was first introduced to the notion of a uniquely American style of capitalism by studying data on entrepreneurship and innovation in the United States. Entrepreneurship is important everywhere, but the United States is a magnet for entrepreneurship like no other country. For example, in a recent ranking of seventy-nine countries on variables including innovation, availability of venture capital, and the share of high-growth firms, the United States ranked first, far ahead of the European Union, Brazil, China, and India, and even ahead of small entrepreneurial countries such as Denmark, Singapore, and Israel.[13]

The United States owes its entrepreneurial success in no small part to the opportunities it has afforded talented and hardworking immigrants. In the global competition for talent, America excels because it provides opportunity both through jobs, which are created by the marketplace, and through education and high-tech research, which are tied to philanthropy. In the United States, 20 percent of high-tech companies were started by immigrants or had immigrants on their founding teams.

At the heart of American-style capitalism—and the ability to attract and sustain entrepreneurial activity—is an acceptance of the cycle of creative destruction. To some, this is a double-edged sword. On the one hand, the forces of creative destruction enable superior innovations to displace old companies and products. This process can also be damaging, however, as the losers in this process are put out of work, and in some cases whole towns and regional economies can suffer. In some countries, government plays an active role in holding creative destruction at bay, whereas American politicians—and presumably voters—have supported a system that allows creative destruction to do its work. Americans seem to accept that although creative destruction creates uncertainty, it also nurtures dynamism and, perhaps most important, fuels the entrepreneurial spirit of American-style capitalism.

The tension in American-style capitalism, thus, is not between the winners and losers that are sorted out by creative destruction. Rather, the tension is between enabling vast amounts of wealth creation for those who innovate and protecting opportunity for all Americans. If government and society put too much pressure on the system from either side, the balance of American-style capitalism could shift in fundamental ways.

Indeed, the growing income inequality in the United States could create lasting cleavages between rich and poor that would do irreparable harm. Among other things, it could damage our meritocracy—our system for allocating talent and good ideas to their most productive uses—which is necessary for a healthy entrepreneurial society. On the other hand, pushing too much on the institutions that enable vast accumulation of wealth could damage the incentive system. As I discuss in this book, philanthropy plays a vital role in easing this tension between encouraging wealth creation and strengthening the institutions of opportunity.

For wealth to invigorate the capitalist system it needs to be "kept in rotation" like the planets around the sun, and for this task American philanthropy is very well suited.[14] Only through philanthropic investments—in particular through the organized, large-scale networks of what I call philanthropic entrepreneurialism—can the imbalance inherent in capitalist growth be corrected to create a self-sustaining process in which wealth creation is supported alongside social innovation and opportunity.

Philanthropists strengthen American-style capitalism in two ways. The first is that philanthropy, when targeted to universities, research, and other productive uses, lays the groundwork for new cycles of innovation and enterprise. As an economist, I understand that it is not always easy to measure the precise contribution that philanthropy has made to economic growth.

What we can be more certain of, however, is that the fruits of philanthropy are all around us, from our hospitals, schools, and universities to our museums, orchestras, and myriad other cultural institutions. Take the Rockefeller Foundation, for example, which is funded by the oil fortune made by John D. Rockefeller in the late nineteenth century. He founded some of America's great research centers, such as the University of Chicago, the Rockefeller University (a medical research center), and the Brookings Institution (a nonpartisan policy research institute).

The second way philanthropy strengthens capitalism is that philanthropy—like creative destruction—provides a mechanism for dismantling the accumulated wealth tied to the past and reinvesting it to strengthen the entrepreneurial potential of the future. Through this recycling process, philanthropy is a partial answer to the question of what to do with wealth, which must be recycled to create social stability and opportunity for those who have to be helped to the starting line. When philanthropy is absent, wealth remains concentrated, rent seeking flourishes, and innovation suffers. Thus, philanthropy plays a much more central role in explaining American-style capitalism than economists recognize.

Philanthropy has the potential to mitigate inequality as it softens the hard edges of the free market. Recycling wealth reduces income inequality and contributes to a more just society. If you leave only money to the next generation, you leave them poor. They will squander it. This was true in the past, and it still pertains to systems that protect the nobility—the major difference between the American experiment and the class systems of old Europe. American philanthropists did not want to leave money to the next generation, as was the tradition in Europe; they wanted to leave opportunity.

It is also important to note that the way in which philanthropy operates is itself entrepreneurial. Philanthropists are innovators of opportunity. They look to where society is most in need—to where they can have the biggest impact—and they create networks and institutions to achieve these goals. Philanthropy is thus consistent with the self-made American values of individual freedom.

One criticism of philanthropy is its lack of accountability, mainly because philanthropists—and the foundations they create to allocate their wealth—do not answer directly to the public. Philanthropy hardly operates in a vacuum, however. To the contrary, over the past century, philanthropy has been bound in a partnership between wealthy Americans and the progressive tides in medicine, education, and civil society.[15]

Philanthropists cannot create sustained initiatives by themselves, but must instead tap into the ready fabric of civil society, medicine, or science to find feasible projects. For example, in founding Rockefeller University—the first biomedical research institute in the United States—John D. Rockefeller did not create biomedical research out of nothing, but instead brought together existing research initiatives and scientific priorities that he believed would honor his legacy.

It would be misleading to argue that philanthropy is the only way in which society contributes to the public good. Government spending—fueled by the taxes it imposes on Americans, particularly the wealthy—also plays a role in reinvesting wealth in opportunity-creating ventures in areas such as medicine, scientific research, and education. In America, however, our model has never been purely about government spending, as it has been in much of Europe.

In part, this has been due to politicians' and voters' resistance to higher taxes and more expansive government involvement in industry and society. Taxes, in particular, have always seemed to Americans to be a necessary evil, largely at odds with the notions of individual freedom, and perhaps as a consequence they have often been infeasible as a policy instrument. Over the past few years, in the wake of the Great Recession, voters' aversion to taxes and the inability of government to act in many policy areas underscore these issues. Philanthropy will never be the only way to invigorate wealth to create opportunity—but it is a necessary part of the American solution.

As the former U.S. president Bill Clinton has pointed out, "There has always been a gap between what the government can provide and what the private sector can produce, a gap charities have long helped to fill. But as our world and economies evolve, we have an opportunity and a responsibility to reconsider how to fill this gap—to rethink the relationship between economic and social challenges, so that benefits and opportunities are available to more people."[16] Philanthropy, whether or not Clinton was aware of it when he wrote that piece, has all along been an unstated principle that lies at the heart of American-style capitalism: that those who amass wealth must continually create opportunities by investing in society. In this book we will explore how most Americans, wealthy and otherwise, historically have exemplified this principle, and reveal the largely hidden role it has played in producing economic growth and prosperity.

The conversation we are having is fascinating precisely because philanthropists are not universally understood or admired. Just think of how some people disliked Bill Gates, just as they misunderstood the "robber barons" Andrew

Carnegie and John D. Rockefeller. Theirs is tainted money! But what if giving wealth away is the key that unlocks future opportunity and prosperity? Giving back does matter, and that is why we are having a conversation about it.

This book is a reflection on contemporary American-style capitalism, with its sharp focuses on the interplay between entrepreneurship and philanthropy, on the one hand, and wealth creation and opportunity, on the other. Using historical and institutional evidence, I trace this story through the centuries. Many philanthropists had humble beginnings, worked hard to make something of themselves, and later used their money to help improve the world. They gave back to the society that had made them successful, thereby helping others make their way successfully along the difficult path of life. The dynamic of American-style capitalism—a self-sustaining circle of opportunity, innovation, wealth creation, and philanthropy—has endured over the centuries.[17]

Our story begins with the founding of the Republic and the way in which Americans forged a new relationship between the dynamic forces of enterprise, wealth creation, and opportunity. The American experiment was built on unprecedented powers of discretion and self-reliance, yet over time these unwieldy forces have also been bound to the common good by the emergence of novel forms of institutional authority and internal restraint. American-style capitalism refers not to the embodiment of a superior political economy but to the idea that our institutions are fundamentally different from those of any other nation.

Institutions are important because they set the rules of the game and determine the incentive structure that influences our behavior. Institutions include any form of constraints that we devise to shape human behavior. They may be formal or informal: tax policy, the rule of law, religion, and so on. Inheritance laws offer a case in point. In France, you must leave your wealth to your family. The United States fought against this convention and changed its laws to allow leaving money to other than family. Institutional constraints include both what individuals are prohibited from doing and under what conditions certain activities may be undertaken, who is punished and who is rewarded.[18]

Yet all is not well in America today. We have two populist political movements under way simultaneously: the Tea Party and Occupy Wall Street. In recent years, political rhetoric has increasingly placed blame on features of American capitalism. John Edwards's description of "two Americas" provides just one example. America may be the first modern country to so successfully unite the dynamism of capitalism and entrepreneurship, but we may also be the first country to oversell the promise of this system. As Warren Buffett explained, "We can rise to any challenge but not if people feel we're in a plutocracy—a state in which the wealth class rules. . . . . We have to get serious about shared sacrifice."[19]

It is by no means clear that the incentive structure for giving, or the attitudes toward humanity, stay in sharp relief in any society over the centuries. Robert Kennedy wrote more than forty years ago that, for "too much and for too long, we seemed to have surrendered personal excellence and community values in the mere accumulation of material things."[20] Are the right incentives in place to elicit good behavior? E. J. Dionne writes, "Thanks to Mitt Romney and such well-known socialist intellectuals as Rick Perry and Newt Gingrich, the United States is about to have the big debate on the nature of modern capitalism that should have started back in 2008."[21] What to do about wealth has put this debate front and center in the American consciousness.

On June 7, 2007, William Henry Gates III delivered the annual commencement address at Harvard. He noted that the focus on financial success among the best and the brightest has left the country devoid of moral role models. Greed has replaced decent conduct, and the American obsession with how to gain wealth has diverted attention from the real question of what to do with wealth. Gates reminded us that in successful societies, as in the sports arena, the goal posts need to be reset periodically to level the playing field. Resetting the goal posts helps the players get better, stronger, and faster, and the equipment becomes more innovative. So, in life as in sports, we now need to reset the goal posts.

Thus, we are left with some final questions: Is American-style capitalism working? Are there changes that need to be made to strengthen the relationships between entrepreneurship and philanthropy and between wealth and opportunity in America? One goal of this book is to consider the policies that can continue to best enable the marriage of philanthropic entrepreneurialism with American-style capitalism. Indeed, in this time of economic turmoil, polarized politics, and divergent incomes, it seems vital to ensure that the entrepreneurial spirit of American capitalism retains its ability to deliver opportunity.[22]

## The Book

This book is written for my fellow economists and social scientists engaged in economic issues, their students who need to understand this, the policymakers they influence, and those in the general public who are interested in their children's future. If our leaders through their advisors are going to forge policies that lead to steady, sustained growth, greater economic equity, and enhanced prosperity, philanthropy is a key, if little-understood, factor. Our institutions that influence philanthropic behavior and the organizations philanthropists build need to be better understood. The rules that influence philanthropy have evolved and need to be better understood to help maximize the positive effects of this distinctive force within American-style capitalism.

American prosperity is often defined in terms of easily expressed statistics, such as GDP and GNP. Such figures allow easy comparison between countries and provide a stable quantitative assessment of how an economy has performed. Yet, the same figures that make comparisons easy also obscure the features of the business and government activity that actually comprises the life of an economy—what gives it strength and vitality. In this book, my goal is to think about American prosperity, not just in terms of GDP but also in terms of some of the key features of the economy that, in my view, have underpinned its strengths and weaknesses. This book is organized around four characteristics of American-style capitalism: opportunity, entrepreneurship and innovation, wealth creation, and philanthropy.

I define these characteristics as currents, like currents in the ocean. Over time and space, currents shift with the changing contours of the ocean floor, shorelines, and other ocean currents. In the context of the American economy, none of the four "currents" I have described is a necessary or sufficient condition for economic growth. Rather, each current has played a vital role in shaping the unique prosperity of the American economy during certain periods in history, often aided by the strength of other currents, but not necessarily. The currents are interconnected, but sometimes the strength of one overshadows another, for better or worse.

The utility of this way of thinking about the American economy is that it allows one to critically examine the nature of the success that the American economy is experiencing at any point. For example, today I would describe the economy as experiencing high levels of innovation, high levels of wealth creation, and moderate levels of philanthropy—in many ways like the Gilded Age at the end of the nineteenth and beginning of the twentieth century. There are, however, questions as to whether the economic system is providing meaningful economic opportunities to all individuals. Thus, there is much to be optimistic about yet there is also room for caution.

The current metaphor provides a roadmap for thinking about each chapter in the context of the book. Chapters 2 through 5 work though each of the four major currents. Chapter 6 brings this analysis together, and chapter 7 assesses these currents in a comparative framework with other major countries in the global economy. Identifying philanthropy as one of the four major currents helps to elevate its importance much more than has previously been done in popular discussions of the American economy and American prosperity.

# CHAPTER 2

# CREATING OPPORTUNITY

[Some Americans define] economic freedom
as an equal chance to become unequal.
—JENNIFER HOCHSCHILD

## Four Thousand Years

For most of recorded history, civilization was pretty easily divided into two classes of people—let's call them lords and peasants. The standard of living of each class did not change very much, and what change did occur was typically not noticeable within one lifetime. The lords generally preserved their wealth by coercion or rent seeking. Lords could choose war and plunder, or they could tax peasants for the use of their property, such as farmland or pastures. Tensions existed between lords and peasants, but if you wanted to move up, you had to stage a revolution.

Some lords were, of course, better off than others—they had more land and more political power—but even the poorest lord had the ability to collect rents because they owned property. Entrepreneurial lords could move up, so to speak, by acquiring more land, but this would require currying favor with those who made decisions about the allocation of land, or it would require staging a revolt against such people. Thus, even though lords had land, they hardly had many opportunities for betterment. Peasants, of course, had it worse. Most were shepherds or farmers and had subsistence livelihoods: all their earnings went either to feeding their families or to paying rent to their landlords. This feudal life changed little until about the 1700s, when technological innovations changed the rules of game: the size of one's landholding began to matter less than what one did with one's land.

The most dramatic changes began in Britain. By the 1750s, a series of agricultural innovations, such as crop rotation and large-scale sheep farming, had revolutionized the productive potential of farmland. Those who were fortunate enough to be born with a title to land could harness these technological insights and pull themselves from the economic malaise of the previous four thousand years.[1] Thus, a wave of agricultural innovations injected a new class into the simplified world of peasants and economically idle nobility—let's call them the upwardly mobile. Throughout the eighteenth and nineteenth centuries, this new class of people would radically transform Britain through innovations that started first in agriculture, but moved to encompass a whole host of modern devices ranging from the light bulb to the steam engine. The revolution in inventing and commercializing these goods started in Britain, but had spread throughout Europe and the Americas by the end of the nineteenth century.

How did the nobility respond to this new class, this encroaching economic rival? In Britain, there were immediate tensions between the idle rich and those who were upwardly mobile. Many of the upwardly mobile were, of course, not exactly nobility, but they did have enough land to adopt and use the new agricultural methods. These changes resulted in the so-called Bloodless Revolution, which gave power to the House of Commons. The idle lords, of course, didn't like giving up power, but they must have realized that they didn't really have a choice. Their monopoly on wealth, which had persisted for so long, had come to an end right before their eyes. Throughout this book, the theme of monopolies will come up again and again as I present examples of types of organizations that have been at odds with opportunity. In Britain, the monopoly on land and wealth held by the richest lords prevented small landlords from improving their lot.

The desire of the British nobility to suppress opportunity—or at least keep a monopoly hold on it—is nothing particular to that island or that time. In Florence during the Renaissance, the House of Medici was an infamous Italian banking family and political powerhouse that was once the richest family in Europe. The Medici were ruthless in their dealings with rival families and other city-states in Italy, such as Milan, Lucca, and Rome, that threatened their power. Although the Medici were great patrons of the arts, supporting Brunelleschi, Michelangelo, and Leonardo da Vinci, the goal of their patronage was not to create opportunity for others but to achieve political power. In fact, the Medici's ruthless cunning inspired Machiavelli when he wrote *The Prince* in 1515. They had a saying: "Money to acquire power and power to keep money." They wanted to maintain their hold on power and limit the opportunity of any other group to challenge this hold.

Even today the impulse persists to limit the opportunity available to those who might do what you do, only better. Consider the rise of capitalism in China over the past thirty years. Beginning in the early 1980s, the Chinese government has progressively allowed free-market activity to take place on the mainland, mainly by designating parts of the country where privately owned companies can move to start businesses. The government has watched this "experiment" closely, monitoring its progress and letting it grow only when it seemed safe to do so. Since the 1980s, China has expanded its experiment, mostly because it has proved very successful economically, but the regime's anxiety persists. Economic empowerment could lead to political change.

## America

The United States, by contrast, never had an idle aristocracy like Britain's. Even the "first families" of Virginia, who were Royalists when they left England and controlled vast plantations in the New World, were inclined to maximize the economic potential of their land. The United States never had a huge state apparatus, like China's Communist regime. The United States did not evolve from a system of warring city-states, in which the economic advances of one family or city were seen as a threat to another. The mass movement of Puritans and Quakers from England in the seventeenth and eighteenth centuries and the relatively egalitarian systems they created in the United States broke down the old class structure that had persisted in Britain. Furthermore, the abundance of natural resources and resulting bounty of economic opportunity brought about new attitudes. In essence, Americans created a system of opportunity in which wealth accrued to those who innovated, not just to those who inherited.

In part as a result of these origins, the economic system in the United States has been comparatively fluid, and has been perhaps best described by Joseph Schumpeter, an economist born in Austria-Hungary (now the Czech Republic) who became president of the American Economic Association in 1948. Schumpeter relied less on mathematics, as is typical of the discipline, than on qualitative insights into the relationships among business, government, and politics. His most critical insight was arguably his articulation of the phenomenon he calls "creative destruction." He writes, "The opening up of new markets, foreign or domestic, and the organizational development from the craft shop and factory to such concerns as U.S. Steel illustrate the same process of industrial mutation—if I may use that biological term—that incessantly revolutionizes the economic structure from within, incessantly destroying the old one, incessantly creating a new one. This process of Creative Destruction is the essential fact about capitalism. It is what capitalism consists in and what every capitalist concern has got to live in."[2] For capitalism to work, he observed, it needed change, which would necessitate the rise and fall of many parts of the economy.

Schumpeter feared, however, that the dynamism of American capitalism—the creative destruction ingredient—was going to be lost. He predicted that large firms would create barriers to entry of other firms—much as the nobility did against peasants—leading to a corporatist state of large firms. The rigidity in this state would bankrupt American capitalism and degrade the American experiment into precisely the type of economic system that it had attempted to avoid. Luckily, Schumpeter's pessimism about the fate of American capitalism has not proved prophetic.

Schumpeter had a good reason to be so pessimistic about the prospect of capitalism in the United States, however. He was writing around the middle of the twentieth century, a time when U.S. industry was controlled by monopolies or oligopolies, many of which had formed during the maturation of the industrial revolution and had consolidated their political power in the decades that followed. For example, there was one major telecommunications company, only three automobile manufacturers, and three major television networks. Many of these were household names like American Telephone and Telegraph, General Motors, General Electric, and Standard Oil. In 1950, regulated monopolies comprised roughly 15 percent of the economy. Those firms that were not directly regulated relied on the various associations and networks, where the largest firms within each industry would coordinate with Washington and seek policies to fix prices and increase barriers to entry. The system could hardly be characterized as dynamic. Yet, all parties preferred this outcome; it was stable and predictable and, for the time being, provided robust economic growth.

Schumpeter's fears were more long-term. Because the system was so static, the opportunity to innovate temporarily disappeared. Economic opportunity for new firms and new ideas—for innovation—was eclipsed.

## Fundamental Tension

Despite the egalitarian origins of America during the early colonial settlement period, the forces of creative destruction and economic growth since then have resulted in uneven allocation of wealth across the population. This is perhaps the fundamental tension in American capitalism: a balancing act between encouraging vast accumulations of wealth and maintaining economic opportunity. As discussed earlier, American capitalism's strength depends on economic opportunity, so that upstart firms can inject innovation into the economy. When this works well, however, a new challenge emerges: vast inequalities in wealth, which threaten to undermine a different, but related, aspect of opportunity. This is not the opportunity to start a new business but rather the ability to participate meaningfully in the economy. If the economy is organized around manufacturing, for example, this would involve the ability to acquire the skills needed for employment on an assembly line. In an economy organized around knowledge creation, it would involve the ability to acquire the tools needed by engineers, computer scientists, and other technically trained professionals.

The extent to which America has succeeded in resolving this tension is openly debated. From a purely statistical standpoint, we know that America is deeply unequal with respect to how income is distributed. On this dimension, America resembles countries in some of the least-developed parts of the world. It is not obvious, however, whether and how this translates to inequality of opportunity. We know that political scientists and psychologists who have examined perceptions of opportunity among the population find evidence of equality of opportunity. A majority of Americans feel as though an individual's economic position is not predetermined by the system—for example, having the system stacked against an individual—but rather is the consequence of the individual's own decisions. Why do Americans have this attitude? Today, perhaps part of the reason has to do with who the wealthiest, and thus most salient, individuals are. For example, looking at the *Forbes* list of richest Americans for some indicator of what it takes to become superwealthy, you find that a majority are self-made billionaires, people who came from middle-class families, worked hard, and were incredibly lucky.

Such perceptions of wealth and beliefs about opportunity in the United States have shaped Americans' ideologies.

Implicit in all of these are narratives about the tension between wealth and opportunity. David Brooks argues that
there are four schools of thought regarding this tension.
On the most conservative end of the spectrum—recently
expressed in the Tea Party movement—are those who want
almost no government role. On the most liberal end are
populists—perhaps most saliently identified today with the
Occupy Wall Street movement—who believe that America
benefits only the wealthy. On the more moderate left are
those who want more government intervention but don't
believe that the system is rigged. Finally, there are the Hamiltonians, who advocate free-market capitalism but believe
that government must play some role to ensure that people
are well equipped to participate meaningfully.[3]

This Hamiltonian ideology characterizes the dominant
forces of capitalism in America: a free-market system, for
the most part, wedded to a commitment to support both
economic opportunity and equality of opportunity. This
commitment is not altruistic; it exists because economic
opportunity and equality of opportunity help keep the
system strong. As I discuss in the following sections, the
government—as an actor in American-style capitalism—
has nurtured a system of progressive opportunity creation
alongside private initiatives, all of which have reinforced a
dynamic and perpetuating system of capitalism.

## Early Opportunity

When people think of the interplay between government
and capitalism in America, they often think of the role that
government programs and policies have played as a countervailing force against capitalism—protecting individuals

from capitalism, not preparing them to harness it. The Progressive movement, the New Deal, and the Great Society come to mind immediately as initiatives that were designed to correct flaws in capitalism or shelter segments of society that did not properly benefit from it. Medicare, Medicaid, Social Security, and other elements of the social welfare state were designed to provide insurance, of sorts, for those who needed it, allowing Americans to pool their risks. These programs provide safety nets so that uncontrollable forces such as sickness, injury, short-term unemployment, and old age do not undermine otherwise strong currents of opportunity for individuals.

Social welfare policies do not propel the capitalist system forward, however; they do not create economic opportunity for individuals by facilitating the accumulation of wealth or sparking entrepreneurial and innovative ventures. These are social safety nets for poor and elderly Americans, and whether or not they should be stronger or weaker is a topic that has been thoroughly explored elsewhere. My focus here will be on education.

Opportunity creation in America has predominately been about education, which has long been linked to the vitality of American capitalism, both in spirit and in practice. Consider the colonial colleges that were established before the Revolutionary War. In many ways, the impulses of American capitalism had already worked their way into these early schools, where sons of traders and merchants acquired Puritan values under the auspices of Congregationalist and Presbyterian religious teachings. These schools were not, however, designed primarily to prepare men for the clergy, although at colleges like Harvard roughly half the graduates would pursue this calling.[4] Instead, these colleges worked to inculcate moral teachings in young businessmen-to-be.

The colonial colleges almost immediately differed from Cambridge and Oxford, after which they were modeled. Oxford University, founded in the fourteenth century, was a religious school that focused on a classical education. Among other things, the Royalist and Anglican influences at Oxbridge were antithetical to the Puritan values of self-restraint and hard work. Students at colonial colleges such as Harvard, Yale, and Princeton typically came from middle-class families in the colonies whose parents sought an education for their sons to provide some grounding in religious learning and preparation for professional life.[5]

Two schools in particular pushed the colonial colleges further in this direction. King's College, which would become Columbia University, announced in 1754 that its curriculum would emphasize surveying, navigation, geography, and history—a far more radical departure from the marriage of aristocracy and Anglicanism that was thriving at Oxford than the colonies had previously witnessed. Ben Franklin's College of Philadelphia, which would later become the University of Pennsylvania, made even greater strides in this direction. In 1756, the college's president proposed that "economic abundance" would require "forming a succession of sober, virtuous, industrious citizens and checking the course of growing luxury."[6] To carry out his vision, the president designed a course of study, approved by Franklin and the college's trustees, that increased the emphasis on practical studies and science.

Over the course of American history, the colonial colleges would continue to adapt and change with the evolving appetites of American capitalism, particularly as the schools were harnessed to the financial largesse of new wealth. But even before the Revolutionary War, the schools were reinventing the relationship between opportunity and education. As the historian Frederick Rudolph puts it in his history of American colleges, "The King's College prospectus of 1754 and the College of Philadelphia's curriculum of 1756 may not have been the first shots in an exchange heard around the world, but they were nonetheless certain indications that the English colonies of North America were beginning to respond not to English needs but to American aspirations."[7]

As the American Revolution receded into history and gave way to the emerging pressures of the industrial revolution, new money and new ideas continued to shape the system of education. Education reformers, industrialists, and technocrats in the nineteenth century were eager to merge the needs of new industrial and agricultural processes with a reinvented system of education. Yet, as Rudolph puts it, "the ordinary farmer and the ordinary mechanic neither sensed the changing nature of their world nor felt any need for training beyond the job itself."[8] This would be yet another "bourgeois" revolution in education, perpetuated by those who saw promise in new seeds and fertilizers that would produce higher yields.

In the late nineteenth century, the agricultural revolution—both in the universities and in the fields—evolved in different ways from state to state. One of the major unifying efforts was the system of land-grant universities that excelled at promoting the "useful arts," such as agriculture, mechanics, and mining.[9] The land-grant universities were so called because of the Morrill Federal Land-Grant Act of 1862, sponsored by Congressman Justin Smith Morrill to support agricultural education. Morrill suggested that colleges in America should "lop off a portion of the studies established centuries ago as the mark of European scholarship and replace the vacancy—if it is a vacancy—by those of a less antique and more practical value."[10] Under the 1862 act, the federal government provided a financial incentive to every state in the union to establish an institution of higher learning devoted to modern agricultural research and education.

This incentive led to crisscrossing public and private efforts. Some states picked private universities, such as Cornell in New York and Dartmouth in New Hampshire. Other states selected their public universities, as Wisconsin did with its university in Madison. And still others created entirely new institutions, such as Texas A&M, which still keeps the "Agricultural and Mechanical" abbreviation that many universities later dropped.

To complement the transformation taking place in the universities, Congress passed the Hatch Act of 1887, which provided federal funds for experimental agricultural research. This largesse contributed to many innovations in agriculture. By the end of the century, new fields of study, including plant pathology, agricultural botany, agricultural chemistry, agronomy, veterinary medicine, and horticulture, had taken hold. There was also great entrepreneurial effort in these systems. The land-grant universities would eventually focus not just on agriculture, but also on engineering in manufacturing and for industrial and military use. Although these developments seem obvious today, at the time they represented a fundamental reinterpretation of the university. Today, every state has at least one land-grant university and seventeen states have two. By midway through the twentieth century, 20 percent of all college students would be enrolled at land-grant universities.

The public university system in Wisconsin is a prominent example. Like many of the emerging universities at the beginning of the twentieth century, the University of

Wisconsin was experimenting with new methods and means of productivity that benefited society. Under the leadership of Charles Van Hise, its president from 1903 to 1918, the university set about innovating and expanding with the stated goal of serving the entire population of the state.[11] Van Hise had obtained an undergraduate degree in mechanical engineering in 1879 and a PhD in geology in 1892, both from the University of Wisconsin at Madison, where he served on the faculty before becoming president. Van Hise supported the traditional roles of preparing undergraduates for work and civic life (teaching) and expanding knowledge (research), but added the third mission of serving the entire population of the state by solving problems and improving health, the environment, agriculture, and the overall quality of life for all citizens of the state.

Driven by Van Hise's vision, the university offered a number of practical and popular extension programs, built leading PhD programs, and forged relationships with policymakers facilitated by the campus's location in the state's capital city. Van Hise thought like an entrepreneur and used commercial terms to explain his goals and methods, likening the university's extension program to a retailer bringing products directly to consumers. Van Hise believed that the university had to "take knowledge to the people and to aid in its application to economic, social, and political problems."[12] The Wisconsin Idea was predicated on the notion that all fields were worth pursuing because, Van Hise believed, "it cannot be predicted at what distant nook of knowledge, apparently remote from any practical service, a brilliantly useful stream may spring."[13]

Today, the "brilliantly useful stream" at Madison still flows. The university enrolls 183,000, on thirteen four-year campuses and thirteen lower-division campuses and extension programs. Returning to the story of the Giving Pledge recounted in chapter 1, it deserves mentioning that the pledge letter written by John Morgridge, the former chairman of Cisco Systems, and his wife, Tashia, reinforces this linkage between American capitalism and education. The Morgridges write that when they left the Midwest in 1955, they were able to pack all their possessions into a 1950 Ford. They continue that they "left the Midwest with much more: with the values, confidence and capabilities learned from our parents, our community, our early public schooling in Wauwatosa, Wisconsin, and from the University of Wisconsin." The Morgridges are now philanthropists, but clearly their background and middle-class values have influenced them in this new undertaking. They continue, "Through hard work, good fortune and the opportunities offered by our amazing country and the world, we have prospered beyond all expectation. As a result, we have been able to add many zeros to the amounts of the checks we are now able to write."[14]

## Institutional Paralysis

It would be impossible to talk about opportunity without discussing the role played by schools and education reformers. In the seventeeth century and earlier, schools were funded at the local level, usually by towns and villages. This practice was so pervasive, especially in the northern parts of the country, that some have estimated that by 1800 the United States had the world's most literate population.[15] This is remarkable considering that it occurred without any state or federal mandate but rather grew out of local, largely democratic, initiatives. This school system certainly did not emerge from the British colonial administrators, who generally made very few educational investments in the New World during this period, even in colonies that generated enormous amounts of wealth, such as those in the Caribbean.[16] Instead, the desire for local schools may have evolved partly from cultural norms in the Puritan and Quaker settlements.[17]

By the early nineteenth century, the more centralized "common school movement," in which state governments actively encouraged localities to develop free schools open to all and paid for by general taxes, had taken hold in the United States. By this time, roughly 90 percent of white adults were literate. Schools developed unevenly under this system, however, and in the worst cases the allocation of spending was intertwined with city politics, which tended to reward supporters of political machines. Education reformers in the early twentieth century broke this parochial hold on education by instituting a national system, a modern coordinated bureaucracy that was more insulated from politics and that could better shift resources to underserved areas. The professionalization of K–12 education was an extraordinary boon to opportunity creation in the United States and has continued to serve many of its basic goals. Today, more than 90 percent of the funding for K–12 education comes from the state, funding that finds its way to more than fifteen thousand school districts across the country, helping to unify curricula and quality standards.

Despite the reach and complexity of the national school system—or perhaps because of it—education has become bureaucratic and resistant to experimenting with innovative reforms that could further improve educational outcomes. Government initiatives—like the land-grant universities— can start out as effective and entrepreneurial solutions to problems. But the efficiencies of scale government initiatives create in bureaucratizing solutions are overshadowed by institutional paralysis over the long run. For decades now, results from numerous international tests have shown that the United States is losing the education race to other countries. As Bill Gates put it, "When I compare our high schools to what I see when I'm traveling abroad, I am terrified for our workforce of tomorrow."[18]

Part of the problem, of course, could be money and that schools are underfunded and teachers are underpaid. As the political scientists Terry Moe and John Chubb put it, however, the problem facing the U.S. school system is largely structural: it has moved away from the beneficial aspects of local control (in which parents have influence) and become too bureaucratic to change. The critical reason for this, according to Moe and Chubb, is that although education benefited from being removed from the damaging influence of political parties by Progressive reformers in the early twentieth century, it now suffers under the control of bureaucrats—that is, teachers and their unions—who resist innovation.[19] In general, government tends to be really bad at creative destruction, even though under the leadership of visionaries like Van Hise it can be innovative.

The major clients of the school system *should* be parents and students, but there is reason to believe that the most influential clients are those who depend on the status quo for their paychecks: teachers, like me. In some sense of the word, I am a bureaucrat; I am employed by the state of Virginia to teach students and conduct research. Although we'd like to believe that most teachers have the best interests of their students in mind, it is also true that teachers care about their own interests, reflected in concern for job security, higher pay, and other workplace benefits. Teachers (or bureaucrats, as I call them) likely have more influence on education policy than any other constituency, and yet, for understandable reasons, they are also the most resistant to change.

Government can be innovative, as the land-grant system and Van Hise's leadership at the University of Wisconsin exemplify. The problem is that, over the long run, the adaptability and innovative drive of public-sector organizations are bound to diminish because there are no incentives to reform. To a large degree, this organizational paralysis that has crept into the public education system possesses the same qualities that Schumpeter feared had crept into the American economy: the inability to adopt new solutions to changing problems and, perhaps most important, to use these innovations to replace what does not work.

## Innovating Opportunity

American industrialists and education reformers have long worked to push the system of education forward, with or without the assistance of government. American capitalism has found ways to perpetuate opportunity both by giving individuals the skills they need to participate and by sowing the seeds of future innovation. Consider first the system of universities in the United States. The role government has played in innovating systems of public education such as the land-grant universities has been met with a sustained parallel role of private philanthropy in innovating systems of private education. Today, a majority of the leading research universities in the United States are private (twenty-three out of the top twenty-five, if you believe *U.S. News and World Report*). Many of these private universities, founded by wealthy entrepreneurs such as Leland Stanford, Johns Hopkins, Andrew Carnegie, and Ezra Cornell, owe their existence to American capitalism. These men built universities to create opportunity for students, often advancing new definitions of higher education to meet the demands of burgeoning industries.

This private system has been propelled, in part, by a sort of feedback mechanism. Capitalism has generated huge amounts of wealth, and this wealth has been, in large part, generated by people with middle-class values who strive to make their mark by helping to maintain a dynamic society. These self-made individuals are entrepreneurial, and their ability to reinvent the industries in which they work has often found a corollary in their innovation in other aspects of the capitalist system, such as the provision of education. Although the philanthropists who funded these universities did not create them, they hired experts to do so. Later we will see, for example, how both Johns Hopkins and John D. Rockefeller did this.

In addition to their goal of educating the workforce, early industrialists recognized that academic research—in theory, and sometimes in practice—can promote innovation in the economy. This has certainly proved true among firms in places like Silicon Valley and in industries like biotechnology and other areas of medical research. Today, many of the United States' best universities, as determined by measures of academic influence, are private. Consider the Academic Ranking of World Universities by Shanghai Jiao Tong University, which focuses exclusively on the research output of universities using measurable observables such as the number of citations of faculty publications in scholarly journals, the number of citations in leading journals like *Science* or *Nature*, and the number of Nobel laureates and Fields Medal winners on the faculty. First, fifty-four of the top hundred universities in the world are located in the United States. Then, of these fifty-four, in 2010 slightly more than half were private. Like the land-grant universities, these private research powerhouses are bound to the capitalist system as they provide not just a skilled workforce but also, increasingly, an innovative breeding ground for new companies.

It is a little unfair to draw a strict division between public and private universities with respect to innovative capacity, however. Many private institutions are heavily dependent on grant money, which comes from private *and* public sources. For example, by the middle of the twentieth century the federal government's support of scientific research had dwarfed private support. In 1949, as the federal effort ramped up, one employee at a foundation complained, "We raised three million dollars for cancer research and then read that the government proposed to appropriate thirty million to the same cause; it's very discouraging."[20] By the late 1950s, one-quarter of Harvard's income each year came from the federal government, and at Harvard Medical School the federal government's share was approximately 57 percent.[21]

Public and private universities have both been active recipients of federal funding from initiatives such as the National Science Foundation. Private philanthropy tends to be dwarfed when the federal government puts it weight behind something. Nonetheless, this ought not to diminish the importance or relevance of private philanthropy, which has been both pathbreaking and corrective, particularly as private universities have injected competition into the allocation of federal largesse.

## Mending Opportunity

Higher education is not the only place where private money has been funneled. Other early capitalists noticed deficiencies in the public provision of K–12 education and created privately funded initiatives to remedy these shortcomings. One of the earliest examples of private giving is that of Stephen Girard, whose Girard College still operates in Philadelphia as a tuition-free K–12 boarding school for children from disadvantaged backgrounds. Girard himself was born fatherless in 1750 and became a sailor at the age of thirteen. He made his fortune by purchasing and operating a fleet of vessels. Robert T. Grimm Jr. provides a good summary of Stephen Girard's life: "During his life, but even more so after his death, people criticized Girard for the harshness of his demanding rationality, his atheism, and his seeming love of property more than people. Yet this man, who became one of the wealthiest Americans of any period in the nation's history, donated much of his time and nearly all of his money to alleviating suffering and encouraging human potential."[22]

During his lifetime, Girard supported many charitable institutions, such as the Society for the Relief of Distressed Masters of Ships and Their Widows, the Public School Fund of Philadelphia, the Pennsylvania Institution for the Deaf and Dumb, and the Orphan Society. In his will, he laid out the mission for Girard College. Girard stipulated that teachers be chosen on the basis of merit and that the students not be taught religion in the school, but rather subjects such as mathematics, experimental philosophy, geography, grammar, reading, and writing. Girard's will was contested by his family but was upheld by the U.S. Supreme Court in a landmark case.[23]

If Girard were alive today, would we call him a social entrepreneur? He noticed a shortcoming in the provision of opportunity and designed a solution to fix it. His innovation still stands and continues to serve underprivileged students in Philadelphia. Girard was also a capitalist through and through and knew what it was like not to have opportunity, remembering the difficulties he encountered in forging his own path to prosperity when he was young. Social entrepreneurship today shares many features with Girard's accomplishment; however, many social entrepreneurs today are not industrialists themselves, but the money on which they rely comes from industrialists and other business magnates. Since Girard's day, these networks of philanthropists and reformers have instituted a separation of labor between the capitalist and the social entrepreneur, although their goals fundamentally remain the same.

Today, if you look around many poor neighborhoods in America, you'll notice there is nowhere for children to play. This is truly unfortunate. When I was growing up in the 1950s in a poor neighborhood in Cleveland, Ohio, we had a playground with swings, a merry-go-round, monkey bars, and basketball hoops. As children we spent countless hours at that playground after school and over the long summers. By contrast, according to the Centers for Disease Control and Prevention, today half of U.S. children live in "play deserts"—neighborhoods without playgrounds, parks, or community centers. Despite a lot of evidence that play is vital for children's physical, emotional, and cognitive development, in recent decades children's outdoor play opportunities have declined markedly. In many poor (and some not so poor) neighborhoods, constrained budgets and

waning taxpayer support have conspired to curtail investments in this resource.

Social entrepreneurs have responded. For fifteen years,
the nonprofit KaBOOM! has been attacking this problem: it
is leading playground construction all over America, mostly
in neighborhoods where at least 70 percent of children qualify for the federal government's free and reduced-cost lunch
program. To finance its vision—an average playground
costs about seventy-five thousand dollars—KaBOOM! has
partnered with large foundations and corporations, including Home Depot (which saw a natural fit with its motto,
"You Can Do It. We Can Help"). Home Depot not only donated cash and materials but also encouraged its associates
to volunteer at "playground builds." KaBOOM's model has
made it a catalyst in repairing the social fabric of disadvantaged communities across the country. The organization
doesn't directly hire contractors to build—which would be
faster and easier—but instead teaches neighborhoods to
organize themselves to turn around their public spaces.
The concept of the "benevolent community"— *e pluribus
unum*, as neighbors pitch in for the common good—is one
of the defining ideals of American history.

In the private market for goods and services, something
that failed to deliver on its promise would be scrapped. But
this is not always the case in government. The incentive for
government to maintain programs—regardless of whether
they work—is too great. Yet, when the country is searching
for policies that are more responsive to economic down-
turns and for a better balance between fighting poverty
and avoiding dependence on its safety-net programs and
between meeting short-term needs and investing in long-
term outcomes, private initiatives have a way of attracting
widespread notice.

In September 2010, Mark Zuckerberg, the founder of Facebook, gave one hundred million dollars to Newark's public schools. The gift initially seemed curious because Newark was far from anywhere Zuckerberg had lived; he'd grown up in Westchester County, a wealthy suburb of New York City, went to college in Cambridge, Massachusetts, and now lives in California. If he'd given the same amount to Harvard, nobody would have batted an eye. So why Newark? As a businessman, Zuckerberg was looking to make an impact with his money. He was drawn to Cory Booker, at that time Newark's forty-one-year-old star mayor, after they met at a conference. On *Oprah*, Zuckerberg remarked, "Newark is really just because I believe in these guys."

With Newark changing, there were plenty of reasons to believe. Just three years into his term as the mayor of New Jersey's long-troubled city, Booker had registered the city's lowest murder rate since the 1950s, doubled affordable housing, and increased pay for city workers—all while slashing the city's deficit. He was known to personally patrol the streets until 4 a.m. and live in a motor home parked near notorious drug corners. His commitment to Newark gained further attention when he turned down President Barack Obama's offer to head the new White House Office of Urban Affairs Policy. Talking with Zuckerberg, Booker shared his next task with him: to tackle Newark's failing public schools, which, despite fifteen years under state control, continued to produce the state's lowest test scores and graduation rates.

One likely way in which the money from Zuckerberg will be spent will be on charter schools. The charter school movement is not private education, as it is an outgrowth of the public school system, but it has been supported by private money and pushed by reformers who are not traditional public school loyalists. The charter school movement is designed to allow competition among schools, which theoretically ought to improve performance. The competition is supposed to spark innovation in teaching methods and improve test scores. In a way, it's the K–12 analog of creative destruction, as parents pull their children out of underperforming schools. Studies, some of which were randomized (the gold standard in scientific research), have shown that this competition is creating effective innovation in some of the poorest and most underserved areas in America.

What is noteworthy about the Zuckerberg story is not the size of the contribution—in 2005, philanthropists gave a combined $1.5 billion to K–12 education, much of which went to charter schools—but that he, like other donors, carefully allocated money to incubate innovative approaches to education reform.[24] John D. Rockefeller had articulated these basic ideas, if somewhat extremely, more than a hundred years earlier in "Some Random Reminiscences of Men and Events": "To help an inefficient, ill-located, unnecessary school is a waste. . . . . [I]t is highly probable that enough money has been squandered on unwise educational projects to have built up a national system of higher education adequate to our needs, if the money had been properly directed to that end."[25]

Educating children and creating opportunity is not about charity. Indeed, a considerable amount of the economic growth in the past hundred years can be attributed, as Tyler Cowen says in his book The Great Stagnation, to educating "smart, uneducated kids."[26] This transformation in the ingenuity and productivity of workers has been critical. More remains to be done, however, to extend opportunity more innovatively and effectively to greater segments of the population, given the evolving demands of the workplace and the economy.[27] As Lawrence Summers wrote, in order to create opportunity for all and combat inequality, "the leading universities must undertake the same commitment to economic diversity as they have towards racial diversity."[28]

## Conclusion

I return now to where this chapter started. The fundamental tension in American capitalism is between the creation of wealth and the maintenance of opportunity. I haven't gone into detail about wealth creation—how America became so rich—which we will consider in the following chapters, but I have discussed the way in which the American system has nurtured opportunity, through both public and private avenues. Indeed, creative destruction, described by Schumpeter as the best aspect of American capitalism, exists also to challenge the institutions that create and nurture opportunity.

One reason the private provision of opportunity—through private universities, charter schools (which, though an outgrowth of the public school system, would not exist without philanthropy), and so on—has been successful in America is demand. If playgrounds across the country were in good shape, projects like KaBOOM! would never gain popularity in neighborhoods. If traditional public schools were delivering adequate results, parents would not want to enroll their children in charter schools. Private initiatives have found plenty of demand in America, however, as a result of a number of troubling recent trends. Over the past few decades, the performance of many public schools has declined, health insurance for workers has become scarcer, the minimum wage has stagnated, millions of jobs have been lost, and prison populations have surged. While these undesirables have been on the rise, the income of the top 1 percent has risen considerably. In many other countries, these trends would stimulate a greater backlash. Indeed, the popularity of extreme-left governments, such as those in Latin America today, is typically fueled by perceived inequality. By contrast, the deep pathologies in the American electorate that make it resistant to taxes and the growth of government have left open avenues for private solutions.

Does the Occupy movement represent a new shift to the left in the United States? Perhaps, though not in any radical way. Far-left governments have never been very popular in the United States, even during periods of great income inequality, such as the early twentieth century. Eugene Debs, perhaps the most well-known socialist in American history, ran for president four times. The first was in 1904, when he received nearly 3 percent of the popular vote, and the last was in 1920, when he campaigned from prison after being found guilty of sedition during World War I and received just over 3 percent of the vote. Around the same time, subscriptions to the major socialist newspaper peaked at about a half million subscribers. Far-left governments never gained mass appeal in the United States, at least partly because voters never believed that the American system was irreparably rigged against them; American capitalism continues to be perceived by voters as being dynamic enough to provide broad opportunities, despite vast inequalities in wealth.

In this chapter, I have described the system of opportunity creation in the United States, which has been a series of inventions and reinventions of the means by which opportunity has been provided. Sometimes these efforts have been spearheaded by the government, as in the case of Charles Van Hise's innovative approach to reshaping the institutional goals of the University of Wisconsin. Other efforts have been both public and private, such as the emergence of charter schools that have challenged the traditional provision of K–12 education in many underperforming school districts. None of the efforts that have shaped the provision of opportunity in the United States have been immune from institutional paralysis, yet the best examples have grown out of consistent and varied pressures to reform and reinvent new approaches.

I have also defined how opportunity has been embedded in American-style capitalism in two fundamental ways. The first is by equipping individuals with the skills they need to participate in capitalism—as the Hamiltonians would advocate. The second relates more to the functioning of innovation and markets, and to the ability of new industries, firms, and jobs to challenge the status quo—namely, creative destruction. The focus of the next chapter is how this latter aspect of opportunity, which has historically been fundamental to the vitality of American capitalism, can flourish.

# CHAPTER 3

# ENTREPRENEURSHIP AND INNOVATION

> The essential point to grasp is that in dealing with capitalism
> we are dealing with an evolutionary process.
> —JOSEPH A. SCHUMPETER

## Why in America?

While I was traveling around the world during the boom years of the 1990s and lecturing on innovation and entrepreneurship (the second current of our story), one question was on everyone's mind: Why did the information revolution—which is sometimes overshadowed by the related dot-com bubble—happen in America?[1] What is unique about this country that made it happen here? My hosts often gave me the short answer: "cowboy capitalism." But when I would ask, "What exactly is 'cowboy capitalism?' "—a phrase associated with Ronald Reagan—my audiences were mostly silent. They could explain Scandinavian egalitarianism: everyone is equal. They understood the Japanese model of a strong bureaucracy led by brilliant planners. And they knew that the German model is a tightly knit social market structure made up of business, labor, and government.

But they had difficulty elaborating on what exactly defined American-style capitalism.

As I have argued, the American model has to do with opportunity, which is fueled by education and knowledge as well as the openness afforded by creative destruction. But what exactly does all this mean and what has it looked like over the course of American history? I've argued that for much of human history, opportunity was fixed; entrepreneurial individuals could not exploit it. The trajectory of American capitalism, however, was rarely fixed—especially not at first. This brings us to our second raging current, entrepreneurship.

The story of how we got to an era of cowboy capitalism starts, to some extent, with the cowboys (or at least an era closer to the time when there were cowboys). It then moves through the twentieth century and explores how the American economy evolved after the settlement of the western frontier. The major changes moved in the direction of large industrial processes and an attitude that, among firms, bigger is better, a period I refer to as the *managerial* economy, which lasted through the 1970s. Finally, the story concludes with the past three decades and considers whether this really is a new era of cowboy capitalism—a shift from the *managerial* economy that dominated for most of the twentieth century to a renewed *entrepreneurial* economy.

Throughout this history, I will keep an ear to the hero of this book, Schumpeter, in order to discern when and where the grinding gears of creative destruction are audible. As mentioned earlier, the American experiment was born out of a hearty acceptance of creative destruction, rejecting less innovative alternatives: feudalism, of course, communism behind the Iron Curtain, and, in much less dramatic ways, regimes and societies that do not embrace economic change and innovation.

The term *entrepreneur* is usually defined as someone who starts his or her own business, typically a small business. When I use the word *entrepreneur*, however, I'm really thinking specifically about those who are developing a new product or business model. Economic growth is fueled by innovative entrepreneurs, not replicative entrepreneurs; growing economies don't necessarily need more dry cleaners but rather more businesses that generate new ideas and new wealth.

## The Physical Frontier

Why does the United States prosper when it does? According to Schumpeter, the function of the entrepreneur is to reform or revolutionize the patterns of production by exploiting an invention or, more generally, an untried technological possibility to produce a new product or to produce an old line in a new way. Of course, entrepreneurs need to be competitive, which requires having good ideas, especially today when they have to work with scientists and engineers. In earlier times, exploiting opportunity was done easily and frequently in the United States.

Many of the workers who came to the United States were entrepreneurial and joined in what was for centuries a largely unmanaged scramble for economic opportunity. In the early days of the country, opportunity was clearly evident in the sheer natural abundance of fish, wildlife, furs, timber, and rich soil. This bounty was there for the taking (although the native peoples had a different perspective). Early settlers made fortunes trading with highly prosperous

Caribbean colonies such as Barbados and Cuba, which had devoted their entire production to sugar and thus were eager to import foodstuffs and other essentials. From the northern colonies came cod, timber, soap, and other surpluses that the relatively small farms accumulated. From the southern colonies came timber, tobacco, and rice. In addition, a certain rebelliousness in the colonies provided the means for rapid wealth creation. By the 1760s, many of the colonies' richest families owed 30 percent to 40 percent of their wealth to the fruits of war, privateering, and piracy.

Later generations of settlers moved westward to exploit new opportunities farther inland, investing in the rich prairies and mineral resources, and the railroads that carried them there. In addition to taking advantage of physical resources, early Americans also built garment factories, saw mills, distilleries, and other cottage industries that lightly manufactured goods and services. These developments introduced new ways of making and distributing goods and services. Many Americans made their fortunes through fur trading, the countless mineral rushes for gold, silver, and other ores, and other speculative enterprises. Sometimes these settlers were innovative and made lots of money, but mostly they were replicative and did all right as well.

Part of what provided the vast amount of economic opportunity for so many early Americans was the distribution of land. In colonial times, for example, the settlements in New England and around Philadelphia were largely influenced by Puritans and Quakers, who did much to dismantle the class system that had kept physical resources so unequally distributed in England. This is not to say that there was no variation in the distribution of land or that some towns—such as New Haven, Connecticut, for example—were not settled in highly unequal ways, but on the whole, the system of land distribution bore little resemblance to that in England. This is a theme to which we return in later chapters. In the southern colonies and parts of Appalachia, however, the distribution of land was more English, with the Virginia "cavaliers" in control of enormous estates that were worked by sharecroppers, indentured servants, and eventually slaves. The obvious benefits of larger-scale production of tobacco and rice, both crops that grew exceedingly well in the southern colonies, also contributed to the preponderance of large plantation farming there.

As the western boundaries expanded, however, the frontier had something of a leveling effect. Frontiersman, whether early trappers and traders or later farmers, largely moved westward in pursuit of economic opportunity. In most cases, such pioneers were neither very poor nor very wealthy; the poor lacked the means to travel and the wealthy lacked the need to risk their fortune on relatively risky settlements. Thus, what bound many frontier communities was a shared sense of middle-class values and a related appreciation for hard work. As Ray Allen Billington and Martin Ridge put it in their treatise on westward expansion, "The frontier has always been identified with the gospel of hard work. . . . . [L]ittle compassion existed for the sluggard, squatter, or drifter. The prolonged siesta, the continental lunch, or the English tea were viewed as intruding on the routine of dedicated labor."[2] The westward expansion was also slow and incremental, with individuals rarely moving more than one state westward in their lifetimes. Thus, families from New England settled in New York, and those from New York settled in Ohio, and so forth.

In the early American economy, opportunity and entrepreneurial activity were mostly tied to the abundance of natural resources, which left fewer incentives to focus on innovation. There were, however, some early exceptions. Benjamin Franklin, for example, who is sometimes nostalgically referred to as the first American, was very much in the "knowledge" business as a successful publisher. Franklin is also known for his inventions, such as the bifocal lens, which he never patented and commercialized. Thus, it is the fortune he amassed as a publisher that most reflects his contribution to America's emerging knowledge economy in the eighteenth century. At the age of twelve, with only two years of formal schooling, he started working for his brother in the printing business, and when his brother founded the American colonies' first independent newspaper, Franklin became a secret contributor under the pseudonym Mrs. Silence Dogood. When his secret was discovered, much to his family's displeasure, Franklin fled to Philadelphia without permission and became an apprentice to yet another printer.

In 1728, Franklin became a partner in a printing house, and a year later became the publisher of *The Pennsylvania Gazette*, in which he raised issues of concern to colonial society. He used comic models to give his newspaper an edge over the competition. In 1730, he was elected the official printer for the Pennsylvania colony. Franklin's paper was very popular, and in 1730 he began to carry advertisements. In 1732, Franklin started publishing *Poor Richard's Almanac*, which sold more than one thousand copies the first year and more than ten thousand copies annually in the following years; almost one person in ten bought a copy. He later moved into publishing novels. In 1749, after twenty years in the printing business, Franklin earned roughly twenty-six times what the average worker earned. This disparity between Franklin's earnings and that of an average worker is nothing in today's context, but it is the beginning of the growing ability of entrepreneurs to amass considerable fortunes. Indeed, to a large degree, the growing inequalities in wealth in colonial America, particularly in the northern colonies, resulted from the ability of some Americans to better exploit the relationship between *knowledge* and commerce.

Stephan Girard, whom we met in chapter 2, made a fortune as an innovative trader during the late eighteenth century. He possessed such specific knowledge of various commodities that he was able to exploit price and quality differentials better than others could. He also had a penchant for smuggling and a knack for getting around trade barriers. Perhaps to his benefit, Girard was hardly the image of the iconic frontiersman. He was short and hunched in stature and suffered from a glaring abnormality in his right eye that brought him ridicule in his early life and left him partially blind. Girard was also a Frenchman who settled in America only in his late twenties, first in New York and then in Franklin's home of colonial Philadelphia. From these flourishing port cities, Girard perfected his trade in goods such as sugar and tobacco and established a commercial empire that linked the Americas with the major ports of Europe and Asia.

The immensity of Girard's wealth is apparent in the fact that by 1811 he was the largest shareholder in the U.S. National Bank, in which he had invested as a business venture. Girard purchased the charter for the First Bank of the United States, and later started the Girard Bank, which was the principal source of U.S. government credit during the War of 1812. When war broke out, the federal government desperately needed funding, which it had to raise without the benefit of a central bank. Treasury secretary Albert Gallatin attempted to borrow money from Girard's bank. At first he did not accept Girard's condition that the bank be placed on an equal status with the public banks, but he did accept the condition that he lobby the Pennsylvania State legislature to make it easier for Girard's bank to grow.

Both Girard and Franklin were innovative; they expanded their businesses, one in publishing and the other in trade and shipping, to levels rarely seen in the colonies. Both also became devout philanthropists, helping to found schools that would prepare future business and professional leaders. Their philanthropic activities will be a subject for later chapters, but for now it is important to note that Girard and Franklin represent an evolution in the way in which wealth was created: wealth came less from land and natural resources than from ways to improve existing systems of commerce.

## The Innovative Frontier

In America, the rush to move west would eventually be displaced by the rush to invent—or to capitalize on inventions. Girard and Franklin died during the onset of America's industrial revolution, when the relationship between innovation and wealth grew beyond anything that their contemporaries would have imagined.

The quickness with which the United States adopted and expanded the technologies of the industrial revolution was in part due to the fluid nature of an economy with virtually no regulatory controls and a political culture that supported competitive enterprise. It also helped that England and parts of Europe had been steadily industrializing for decades, allowing for easy adoption of many technologies. Take, for example, the race to provide affordable lighting. In 1784, a Swiss inventor and Enlightenment philosopher named Francois-Pierre-Ami Argand invented a central draft lamp (an invention for which he was never properly credited). It caught on and by the mid-nineteenth century was a staple in households rich and poor.

Yet, by the time Argand's lamps were in widespread use, gas lighting had become mainstream. The first gas lighting of public streets took place along London's Pall Mall in 1807, and the first gas company in the world came into being in 1812. The New York Gas Light Company was founded in 1923 and began installing gas pipes throughout the city to light homes and streets. These replaced many of the whale-oil-burning lamps, like Argand's, that had been in use in New York City since the mid-eighteenth century. Yet, soon after the gas lighting industry replaced earlier technologies and secured a monopoly in many cities, it faced its own existential crisis.

In 1879, the industrious American inventor Thomas Edison demonstrated that electricity could generate enough light to provide a better and cheaper alternative to gas. After thousands of attempts working with carbon and bamboo filaments, he perfected a light bulb that would burn seemingly endlessly and was granted a patent in 1880. Existing gas companies recognized the threat. In New York, the heavily consolidated gas industry essentially used its monopoly rents to buy out smaller suppliers of electricity, thus ensuring that it would become a gas *and* electric company. Edison, by contrast, continued to make further innovations in the transmission and distribution of electricity and would found the Edison Electric Light Company with backing from financiers such as J. P. Morgan. Edison declared, "We will make electricity so cheap that only the rich will burn candles."[3] Edison's company would go on to become General Electric, a staple of the American economy ever since.

The story of light is one simple example of the American experience with the knowledge economy. The scientific, technical, and organizational advances of the later nineteenth century represented an era of great opportunity. During the early part of the industrial revolution, entrepreneurs took advantage of new organizational constructs to build financial empires based on the movement and manufacturing of natural resources. Captains of industry were able to amass great fortunes, both by seizing on the new demand for extractive resources and by quickly understanding how technology was changing the opportunities for transportation.

Andrew Carnegie is emblematic of this period. He was born in the town of Dunfermline, Scotland, the first child of a weaver. His father was not able to cope with the technological changes in his craft—from the hand loom to the stem loom—and the family struggled to survive. Andrew, who was not interested in school, helped his mother keep accounts for the family business. He was thirteen when they moved to the United States, where he worked in a cotton mill while learning bookkeeping at night school. Carnegie went on to create the modern steel industry and became, by some measures, the fifth richest man in U.S. history.[4]

Like Franklin, Carnegie had a passion for reading and learning, and he was encouraged in his pursuits by an uncle and other mentors. He also wrote for newspapers and published anonymously. Carnegie took a job as a telegraph messenger and was soon promoted to telegraph operator. While working at the telegraph office, he met Thomas Scott, the superintendent of the Pennsylvania railroad, and soon went to work for him as a clerk and telegraph operator. Carnegie accepted the job in 1853 for a salary of thirty-five dollars a month.

The American Civil War was the first modern war in which major technological advances in warfare, including ironclad ships, were deployed. During the Civil War, Carnegie was called on to help build military roads and telegraph lines and to keep communication open between North and South. He was also instrumental in keeping the railroads running, building iron bridges where wooden ones were not adequate. Carnegie set up iron mills and steel plants to ensure the production of high-quality materials. He introduced accounting into iron mills management, which enabled him to track costs at each stage of production and gave him insights into what each employee did, who was saving materials, and who had the best results, all of which helped him identify waste and increase profits.

In 1875, Carnegie realized that iron would soon give way to steel, as steel was stronger and more flexible. This led to a "steel revolution" in the United States, which was the first country that had all the raw materials needed to produce steel. By the end of the nineteenth century, the Carnegie Steel and U. S. Steel companies were the largest producers of steel in the world. Carnegie eventually sold his company to J. P. Morgan for $480 million.

By the time Carnegie got out of the steel business in 1901, the western frontier had been almost completely closed and access to free natural resources had become much more limited. This development in the availability of opportunity, as suggested by the historian Frederick Jackson Turner, raised the question of whether America and its institutions would endure. In fact, the frontier only shifted further in the direction that innovators like Franklin and Girard had moved, from a physical frontier to an intangible frontier of knowledge creation. Indeed, further inventions took American capitalism on new turns at the beginning of the century, entering a much more intense phase in the use of resources and the creation of knowledge. Innovations such as Ford's assembly line and the creation of large manufacturing plants, for example, put many of the smaller and more decentralized manufacturing shops out of business. The displaced workers, plus immigrants and farmers, flooded urban centers in New York and Chicago looking for opportunity in the new centers of American capitalism.

## The New Institutions of American Innovation

The radical changes in the economy during the agricultural and industrial revolutions also ushered in new ways to innovate, especially from an organizational perspective. New initiatives manifested in three different sectors. In business, emerging giants of industry such as Bell, Xerox, and others built their own research laboratories, which were largely funded by these companies' near-monopoly control over their industries. In education, large universities evolved to take on research in the sciences and engineering. In government, federal policies heightened the importance of science on the national agenda, both for war and for security, as well as for promoting national prosperity.

Today, when one thinks of innovation in the United States, highly visible technology start-ups like Google and Facebook often come to mind. One might also think about America's research universities such as Stanford and Harvard, where scientists work on pathbreaking projects in fields like genomics and robotics. In the mid-nineteenth century, there was nothing in the United States that resembled this from an organizational standpoint. Obviously technology was in a very different place, but companies did not yet have in-house research departments, as Google and Facebook do, nor did universities focus on much more than teaching undergraduates. In 1880, Harvard had only forty-one graduate students. By the close of the nineteenth century, however, much of the modern organizational structure for innovation would take shape under the weight of new capitalist endeavors.

In chapter 2, I discussed the growing role of research universities in starting the agricultural revolution. Many of the new technologies in seeds, fertilizers, and machinery were developed at state land-grant universities, where public and private money were used to innovate a modern agricultural economy. In general, these research universities offered agricultural and technical education to students while developing new technologies that could be applied directly on farms. Fields such as agricultural botany, agricultural chemistry, agronomy, and veterinary medicine resulted. This reconceptualization of the university as an economic innovator was revolutionary in a time when "traditional" colleges like Harvard had little interest in basic research. The turn of the century was a transformative time, however, and universities that had nothing to do with agriculture would also undergo changes. It is in this period that a wave of education reformers and wealthy capitalists like Johns Hopkins and Ezra Cornell built and reshaped universities to focus more on research and knowledge, not just in fields like agriculture but across the range of human discoveries.

By the mid-twentieth century, the research university in the United States would prove more important for economic prosperity—probably much more than its early advocates ever realized. During the industrial revolution, as incubators of new technologies these nascent institutions were still just background players. Companies and inventors took the lead in establishing research facilities to work on new projects. The prototypical model was Menlo Park, Thomas Edison's research laboratory. When Edison was a young man in the 1870s, no university had the facilities he needed to conduct his research. Therefore, out of necessity he built what would become the country's first industrial research laboratory.[5]

In 1876, Edison built the Menlo Park Laboratory in New Jersey, twenty-five miles south of New York City. (Coincidentally, 1876 also witnessed the founding of Johns Hopkins, which would become the first modern American research university.) Menlo Park was quickly furnished with the finest scientific equipment and devoted to invention for the sake of innovation. Edison's objective was to have all of the tools, machines, instruments, and materials in one place for his research. At this time few universities had research laboratories, and those university research labs that did exist were poorly equipped. Edison had fine scientific instruments, including an expensive reflecting galvanometer, electrometer, and photometrical devices.[6] Indeed, one key to the success of Menlo Park was that Edison invested more technological and financial resources in innovation than anyone had previously. Edison held more than one thousand patents and was responsible for inventing the electric light bulb, electric power distribution, and the phonograph, and improving telephone, telegraph, and motion picture technology. He also founded numerous companies, which catapulted him into an elite club of early twentieth-century millionaires.[7]

Like Edison's Menlo Park laboratory, research facilities were integral to the major corporations of the industrial age: General Electric, DuPont, B. F. Goodrich, Kodak, RCA, and IBM all built industrial research laboratories. Most of the industrial research laboratories in the chemical, petroleum, electrical, and rubber industries were founded before World War II. Bell Labs became the preeminent model, at its peak employing twenty-five thousand people; the research conducted there has led to thirty thousand patents and six Nobel Prizes. Among its premier inventions are the transistor, cellular mobile telephony, sound motion pictures, and stereo recording. Between 1921 and 1946, the employment of scientists and engineers in industrial research laboratories in U.S. manufacturing industries grew from 2,775 to 45,941. Five states dominated this activity: New York, New Jersey, Pennsylvania, Ohio, and Illinois, together employing 70 percent of those scientists and engineers. With this unprecedented centralization of invention, it's safe to say that most innovations in this period came from large established businesses, many of which were monopolies or oligopolies in their industries.[8]

The federal government also played a major role in spurring innovation, although this effort was always subject to the vicissitudes of political goals. During the agricultural revolution, the government provided funds for scientific research through programs like the Hatch Act. A number of other smaller initiatives were also at play, but it was not until World War II that the federal government stepped up its involvement. Elites in the postwar era understood that innovation was important for economic growth, but national security would be the main driver. The looming threat of Soviet attack during the Cold War ramped up the government's interest in scientific knowledge. In a matter of decades, an unprecedented amount of money was invested across government agencies and in universities. In fact, federal government funding helped propel so-called private institutions such as Stanford, Johns Hopkins, and the University of Chicago to academic stardom.

Initially, World War II had an important role in shaping the trajectory of federal involvement in innovation. Total federal research expenditures increased sixteen-fold during the five fiscal years that the United States was at war. Over the same period, the research expenditures at the Department of Defense increased about thirteen-fold. The success of the federal Manhattan Project created several important legacies. First, it created faith in hard science to deliver innovations. Second, it contributed to an optimistic postwar perception of the possibilities of large-scale science for the advancement of social welfare.

With the potential seen in scientific research, the federal government took its model of funding land-grant universities mainstream; the creation of the National Science Foundation and the National Institutes of Health in the 1950s reflected a desire to support a university model of research. Before the war, support for university research totaled less than a half billion dollars, spread across private and public institutions. This quadrupled by 1960. The infusion of funds transformed major American universities into centers of scientific research, a role to which many of them had never previously aspired. In the 1950s, federal agencies contributed an average of about 70 percent of the vastly expanded university research budgets. Universities and private foundations each contributed another 9 percent and industry contributed most of the remainder.

In 1957, the Soviet Union launched Sputnik, the first artificial satellite, into earth orbit. The launch, which took the United States by surprise, precipitated a crisis leading to the space race between the two superpowers. The Sputnik crisis provided the leaders of academia with a window of opportunity during the Eisenhower and Kennedy presidencies.[9] The President's Science Advisory Committee enjoyed a half decade of high visibility and successful policy advocacy. Between 1958 and 1963, federal policymakers made two historic decisions: first, that the federal government would assume *primary* responsibility for supporting basic research in the United States, and second, that the research enterprise would be carried out predominately by the nation's universities as an integral component of graduate education. In just ten years, federal support for basic scientific research increased by 50 percent, the federal budget for research overall increased 250 percent, and federal funding of university research grew by 455 percent. Much of this research focused on military applications, although some of these "big science" projects resulted in products that had civilian uses—prime examples include computers, jet engines, radar, and penicillin.

During the 1960s, the federal government's innovative thrust started to falter. As egalitarian populist pressures increased in the 1960s, the Kennedy and Johnson administrations responded by retaining the core formula of funding universities but made three major changes. First, agencies were directed to widen the geographic distribution of federal research support, emphasizing physical facilities and attempting to double the number of strong research universities. Second, federal research support was extended to the social sciences, the humanities, and the visual and performing arts. Third, federal support was significantly expanded, extending beyond the roughly one hundred doctorate-granting universities to provide funding for construction and nonscientific programs, including student financial aid, to more than three thousand institutions. These included community colleges, private liberal arts colleges, state colleges and regional universities, historically black institutions, and vocational and proprietary schools. Thus, on the Great Society agenda, federal science policy expanded and blurred into higher education and social policy. Nonetheless, the basic model of university-led research continues to provide a powerful force in incubating new technologies.

## The Managerial Economy

The late nineteenth and early twentieth centuries were a period of incredibly rapid invention and commercialization. The new business elites claimed their thrones, displacing many of the smaller businesses that had come before them. The enormous changes in production and commerce that took place during this revolution changed the physical makeup of the economy in ways that would go unchallenged for nearly a century. Of the companies on the 1994 list of the *Fortune* 500, 247 had been started in the period from the 1880s through the 1920s. Many companies that are household names, such as Ace Hardware and Disney, were started in the early twentieth century, before the Great Depression.

In many ways, the entrepreneurial forces that had defined America from its early years through the industrial revolution withered in the postwar period; the entrepreneurship of previous centuries grew into the static corporatism of midcentury America. This was driven in part by an allegiance to a "bigger is better" model of economic thinking, which had influential adherents not just in business but also in government and academia. Indeed, American corporatism would be sustained by politicians, bureaucrats, and regulators as much as by business itself.

In 1911, Schumpeter's essay *The Theory of Economic Development* proposed a novel explanation of entrepreneurship and innovation. For Schumpeter, the entrepreneur is a key figure in the economy, "quite simply . . . . the personal cause of economic development."[10] Schumpeter argues that the entrepreneur is the mechanism of economic change and development. Inviting the entrepreneur into the "system" unleashes a vital energy that propels it. In a Schumpeterian world, the routinized social hierarchy, static corporatism, is creatively disrupted by the gifted few.

When Schumpeter wrote his essay in 1911, it seemed apt to describe the dynamism in the economy. Thirty years later, however, Schumpeter's optimism about the entrepreneur and American capitalism had waned. In 1942, Schumpeter predicted a slowdown in innovation and productivity as a result of the hegemony of the large firm. In his best-known book, *Capitalism, Socialism and Democracy*, Schumpeter wrote, "The perfectly bureaucratized giant industrial unit not only ousts the small or medium-sized firm . . . . it ousts the entrepreneur and expropriates the bourgeoisie as a class which in the process stands to lose not only its income but also what is infinitely more important, its function."[11] That is, big business can have a deleterious effect on entrepreneurship.

In the 1950s, *Fortune* magazine wrote that the "huge publicly owned corporation . . . . has become the most important phenomenon of mid-century capitalism." Reporting on its public opinion research, it commented, "Corporate bigness is coming to be accepted as an integral part of a big economy."[12] Many academics held similar views and expressed, at best, ambivalence about the size of firms. In 1926, Keynes wrote, "I believe that in many cases the ideal size for the unit of control and organization lies somewhere between the individual and the modern state."[13]

Certainly, however, some of the innovations that typified the entrepreneurial times of the late nineteenth and early twentieth centuries relied on large-scale production. Henry Ford's assembly line was predicated on the need to have large factories for efficiency gains. Other manufacturers of course followed suit and, before long, instead of competing through innovation, firms competed by trying to outgrow one another without fundamentally altering anything about their business models. The result was stalemate, both for the firms and for the forces of creative destruction.

As Robert Reich notes in *Supercapitalism,* "Steel was controlled by three giants—United States Steel, Republic, and Bethlehem; the electrical equipment and appliance industry by two—General Electric and Westinghouse. In basic chemicals, there were three—DuPont, Union Carbide, and Allied Chemical. In food processing, three dominated— General Foods, Quaker Oats, and General Mills. In tobacco, three—R. J. Reynolds, Liggett & Myers, and American Tobacco; in jet engines, two—General Electric and Pratt & Whitney; in automobiles, three—General Motors, Ford, and Chrysler. In the new industry of television broadcasting, there were three networks—NBC, CBS, and ABC." Similar types of consolidation were seen across American industries.[14]

During the postwar period the extended conflict with the Soviet Union and a profound hatred of the Communist ideology characterized politics. From an economic standpoint, however, it is interesting that the model of megacorporations that the United States adopted resembled in key ways the planned economies of socialist and communist countries. Under socialism—and perhaps even more so under communism—the entrepreneurial function of society is no longer needed.

The dominant view under these systems of government was that bigger was better. Rigid adherence to this principle was embedded in the communist model, as any deviation from mass production was viewed as wasteful. This belief in economies of scale dated back at least to Karl Marx, who expected it to lead to a "constantly diminishing number of the magnates of capital, who usurp and monopolize all advantages of transformation." The ultimate state, he wrote, is one in which "the entire social capital would be united in the hands of a single capitalist."[15] Lenin was similarly obsessed with the efficiencies of large-scale production, as was Stalin in later years.

Although it's true that there was something beneficial in the efficiency gains of an economy dominated by large firms, there were also some undesirable consequences— many of which were unintended. One of the outcomes of this "big is better" period was that the relationships among businesses in the same industry and between business and government grew too cozy. Firms didn't need to compete if they could collude, and collusion was easy when there were only a few players. Government could have intervened to stop this collusion and stimulate competition, but it rarely did. Instead, when government did get involved (for example, to impose regulatory controls on industry), it tended to work too closely with business and the two formed partnerships, both implicit and explicit, that had dire consequences for innovation and entrepreneurship.

Consider the story of a strange but potentially useful device called the Hush-A-Phone, a 1940s innovation introduced by an inventor-entrepreneur duo during the heyday of Bell's influence over all things related to the telephone. The Hush-A-Phone, a large plastic cone that attached to the mouthpiece of a standard phone, acted as a phone silencer. It used sophisticated acoustics to make one's voice less audible to those in the room. The device was perfect for busy offices where workers sat side by side answering telephones all day. To Bell, however, the Hush-A-Phone was a small but uncomfortable threat to its complete control over the industry. Government regulation at the time was supportive of Bell's position. A Federal Communications Commission (FCC) regulation read, "No equipment, apparatus, circuit or device not furnished by the telephone company shall be attached to or connected with the facilities furnished by the telephone company."[16]

Under this clause, the makers of the Hush-A-Phone were ordered to stop production and sale of their product, and they were taken to court. After an extended five-year ordeal, the Hush-A-Phone was ruled illegal by the FCC, despite being shown to be effective, safe, and popular—the company claimed to have sold a quarter million units before being ordered to stop. After a lengthy appeal, the company was eventually vindicated, but by this time Bell was close to putting out a new type of phone for which the Hush-A-Phone would have to be remodeled, and legal fees had nearly bankrupted the company. A few years after the appeal, Hush-A-Phone folded.

Somewhat ironically, government first started to intervene in the economy to break up monopolies, which were blamed for a number of economic and social problems. Competition, of course, is a natural force for inducing firms to innovate, because the only way to win is to make products better and more cheaply than your rivals. Business formed close relationships with government, either as managed monopolies or as trade associations working with regulatory agencies and Congress. The main policy goal of trade associations and managed monopolies was to reduce competition for existing firms and to provide predictability in the market. Thus, government aided large firms by managing the economy. Roughly 15 percent of the economy was managed directly through monopoly regulators, and the rest was indirectly managed through relationships between government and large firms representing whole industries. The dominant policies pursued were those that limited competition. Diminished competition led to greater economic predictability, which had perks as well. Employees who were considering taking jobs with IBM in the postwar period were told to discuss the matter with their wives because "once you came aboard, you were a member of the corporate family for life."[17]

The culture of large firms pushed away from innovation. Economic concentration begins to have a negative effect on entrepreneurial values, innovation, and technological change. Technological change, the means by which new markets are created, and the creative destruction needed to create opportunity are both reduced to a crawl. The United States was able to ride out the technological innovations that occurred during the industrial revolution, and it could coast on this wave for a considerable period because there was no competition. Observers thought that firms would continue to get more efficient doing what they had always been doing, and new markets domestically and overseas would continue to be exploited. The specter of globalization and renewed competition had not yet undermined the managed economy.

## Evidence of Decline

The opening shot was fired by Norman Macrae, the deputy editor of *The Economist*, in 1976. In an article on December 25, "The Coming Entrepreneurial Revolution: A Survey," he suggested that, in the next few decades, business was going to change radically in a direction that most businessmen and politicians did not expect. He predicted that the era of big business was drawing to a close.

Big business would not be replaced by state capitalism, he argued. Bureaucratic production cannot work because its managers will not introduce labor-saving technologies. The problem is that educated people in the rich countries do not want to be organized from the top down. When people can talk to a friendly computer (he wrote this before the PC and email), we will find a surplus of entrepreneurs that will start their own businesses. Norman continued, "This is exactly what is needed to take advantage of tomorrow's technologies. . . . . At a time when the appearance of so many alternative new technologies should make an increase in entrepreneurship so desirable and such potential fun . . . . rich countries will be silly if they restrict entrepreneurship to the few brave fanatics who can take imprudent risks."[18]

How do we then manage in a world where you cannot tell people what to do? As the management guru Peter Drucker pointed out, "You have to learn to manage in a situation where you don't have command authority, where you are neither controlled nor controlling. That is the fundamental change." And how should we live our lives? He suggested, "Corporations once built to last like pyramids are now more like tents. . . . . You can't design your life around a temporary organization."[19]

In August 1980, the *New York Times* ran a series of five stories titled "Reviving Industry: The Search for a Policy." After a decade of hearing about the macroeconomic problems of inflation and unemployment, it was unusual to be confronted with a set of "micro" problems.

The first story, "U.S. Industry Seeking to Restore Competitive Vitality to Products," pointed out that the United States, which had been the envy of the world in the immediate postwar period, could no longer hold its own against Japan and Western Europe.[20] The second story, "Depressed Industrial Heartland Stressing Urgent Need for Help," focused on the condition of a traditional core industry—steel—in the Ohio Valley. The difficulty faced by the steel industry simply would not go away, and after a decade of problems it was on the verge of collapse. It suffered from plant closings, lack of international competitiveness, capital shortage, inadequate investment, and high unemployment. It was argued that if a way could be found to save the steel industry, it would save the U.S. economy.[21]

The third story, "Amid Stagnation, High Technology Lights a Path," highlighted the fact that while some sectors of the U.S. economy were in decline, others were full of vitality.[22] The information revolution was under way and growing industries included computers, office machinery, drugs, communication equipment, electronics components, aircraft, and semiconductors. These industries were the result of the entrepreneurial renaissance.

The fourth story, "Can Japan's Aid to Its Industry Guide U.S.?" wondered whether, if the Japanese government could improve the workings of Japan's economy, our government could improve ours.[23] The fifth story, "Carter Economic

Renewal Plan," discussed industrial policy. The most interesting question was how much help to give the old industries and how much should go to high-tech industries.[24]

While factory after factory closed in the great industrial heartland of America—the great deindustrialization—Japanese goods were pouring into the United States. The Japanese were successful not only in exporting steel, tires, motorcycles, automobiles, and electronics but also in the very core of high-tech industry.

Yet, one of the great engines of American postwar prosperity, the steel industry, as it struggled in the face of increased competition from Japan and Germany, was evolving in the 1970s. While U. S. Steel and Bethlehem Steel were closing plants, laying off workers, and losing money, new steel plants based on new production methods were thriving, ultimately to become known as the "mini-mills" of the American steel industry. How was that possible? They didn't follow business as usual but instead innovated by applying new ideas to the production of steel.[25] A shift in entrepreneurial initiatives was occurring across the industrial landscape.


## The Information Revolution

At the same time the *New York Times* was lamenting the stagnation in the economy, promising new forms of organizational development were emerging; in short, the managerial economy was giving way to an undercurrent of innovation. Across a number of industries, smaller firms were developing more innovative and game-changing products than their larger competitors were.[26]

Perhaps emblematic of this change was the rise and fall of IBM, which had in the 1970s been the undisputed leader in computing. IBM's business of leasing large mainframe computers to companies helped skyrocket the relatively small firm to *Fortune* 500 status in the 1950s, putting it in the ranks of companies like Remington Rand and General Electric. IBM pioneered a number of innovations that made mainframe computers more accessible and customizable for large companies. To computer consumers today, these machines would have looked like large refrigerators stacked side by side, connected by crisscrossing wires; in its day, however, IBM was the state of the art. By the 1970s, IBM *was* computing.

The huge scale of IBM's research budget bears special mention. In the 1950s, its research and development costs were around 35 percent of the company's net income. By the 1960s and 1970s, IBM was investing half of its net income in developing new products. IBM was actually investing more money in computing research than the federal government was. Arguably, IBM really could not have been investing more in development of new and innovative products, yet its efforts would still not be enough to fully take advantage of the technological changes that were on the horizon. Most people would have found this unimaginable in the 1970s, when IBM's dominance in the computer industry was undisputed, with annual sales around seven billion dollars. IBM's dominance in computing resembled the dominance in their industries of companies like Standard Oil and U. S. Steel in their heyday. Yet, despite IBM's firm footing, the company would struggle to cope with changes in the economy that would displace the need for its mainframe computers.

Other large companies in the 1970s would also struggle to get a handle on the new developments in computing technology. The legendary Xerox PARC, or Palo Alto

Research Center, was like the Bell Labs of the West Coast: large, chock full of scientific brilliance, and given considerable autonomy to pursue the kinds of projects it wanted, independent of Xerox's core business model. Xerox could afford to have such a miraculous facility thanks to its near monopoly on the office photocopying machine. Xerox PARC, among other inventions, was responsible for the first *personal* computer, which was invented in 1972 and named "Alto." It was no IBM mainframe but rather a smaller machine with a microprocessor and software. Decades later, when Steve Jobs sued Microsoft for stealing the "look and feel" of Apple's graphical user interface, Bill Gates retorted that both of them had stolen the idea from Xerox PARC.

Research institutes like PARC were incredible places to spark inventions; what could be wrong with laboratories filled with the finest minds in science and engineering? But these corporatist incubators were wholly unsuited to capitalism—the creation and accumulation of wealth. Xerox was never really interested in exploiting many of the inventions that PARC was churning out. It did make billions from the laser printer, which came out of the research laboratory, but in general PARC was too fast and too radical for Xerox's established corporatism.

IBM's bureaucratic nature would also be a liability as it tried to adapt to the technological changes that were happening outside of its research department. In 1981, IBM did come out with a model personal computer, radically transforming its product line from the old mainframe computers. This was an impressive accomplishment, but it was not wholly an IBM accomplishment. In order to build the personal computer, IBM became more dependent than ever on smaller suppliers of the computer's component parts. Two notable examples are the microprocessor, which IBM purchased from the newly emerging company Intel, and the operating system, which IBM commissioned Bill Gates and Paul Allen to develop. Thus IBM was able to pull together a personal computer for the market, but the real innovations—the software and the hardware—came from start-ups that later would far surpass IBM.

With the manufacturing of personal computers, IBM had the dominant model on the market for a while, but soon other companies caught on to what IBM was doing. Michael Dell started assembling computers in his University of Texas dorm room as a college student in the mid-1980s. He thought he could make a cheaper product than IBM's, and he was right. In 1992, at the age of twenty-seven, he became the youngest person to have his company ranked in the *Fortune* 500 list. In 2001, Dell computers had 12 percent of the global PC market. As of 2012, Michael Dell is worth nearly sixteen billion dollars and is the eighteenth richest person on the *Forbes* 400 list and the forty-first richest person in the world.[27]

People like Bill Gates and Michael Dell were typical of much of the new culture in the computing industry. Both were young and industrious and recognized that new ideas and firms could revolutionize their industry. Gates did not believe that one needed to have a research budget that rivaled the federal government's, as IBM did, in order to be a player. In his mind, and in the minds of many of his contemporaries during the information revolution, the American economy was wide open.

Bill Gates was born in Seattle, Washington, in 1955 to a prosperous middle-class family. His father was a successful lawyer and his mother a schoolteacher. Gates had been interested in computers since his high school days, when he wrote his first program—for a game of tic-tac-toe. In his sophomore year, Gates devised an algorithm for pancake sorting as a solution to a number of unresolved computing problems. His solution held the record for thirty years and was later formalized and published with Christos Papadimitrio, a Harvard professor.

By 1975, once Intel had developed the microprocessor, Gates and his high school friend Paul Allen were already writing code. Over the next few decades, the computer industry would be changed by a wave of middle-class programmers, engineers, and entrepreneurs like Gates and Allen, many of whom would make millions, if not billions.

## Innovation in Large and Small Firms

The technological innovations that propelled the computing revolution present the most dramatic example of the forces leading to the breakdown of the managerial economy.[28] Small firms driving innovation led to similar changes in industries across the country. In a series of studies in the late 1980s, David Audretesch and I examined the innovative output of large firms and small firms founded by entrepreneurs in the United States. Looking at thousands of innovations across hundreds of industries, we found that large firms were still responsible for innovation in some industries, but entrepreneurial firms were responsible for innovations in others.

Perhaps most striking, in electronics and computing equipment—the heart of the high-tech revolution—we found 395 innovations, of which large firms accounted for 158 and entrepreneurial firms accounted for 227 (with an additional 10 coming from firms of unknown size). On a per employee basis, the small entrepreneurial firms were more than twice as innovative as large firms.[29] Although most innovations occurred in high-tech industries dominated by a few large firms, most of the innovations in those industries were coming from new entrepreneurial firms. A second line of research found that most of these entrepreneurial firms were clustered in Silicon Valley and Boston's Route 128.

The share of small firms in manufacturing began to grow, reversing the trend toward larger firms during the previous one hundred years. Some indicators of entrepreneurial activity also began to change. The number of self-employed people outside of agriculture plummeted from 1966 to 1968 and then recovered slowly, reaching its previous level only in 1978, rising slowly until about 1990, and remaining roughly constant since then.

The number of businesses per one thousand people, which had declined steadily since 1948, leveled off around 1970. New business incorporations started to increase in the late 1960s. The number of IPOs was low in the 1960s, but rose temporarily to a much higher level in the early 1970s, only to fall to extreme lows in the latter half of the 1970s.[30] With the arrival of the microprocessor and recombinant DNA as well as higher oil prices in the early 1970s, additional forces were set in motion. The industrial giants were no longer able to absorb the new technologies, and new mechanisms and new institutions were needed.

Politicians in the United States have been very supportive of these changes in the economy, across both political parties. This should not be surprising, of course, because the new firms were innovative, bringing new technologies to market and creating enormous wealth. Consider the words of Ronald Reagan in a May 1988 speech to students at Moscow University: "The explorers of the modern era are the entrepreneurs, men with vision, with the courage to take risks and faith enough to brave the unknown. These entrepreneurs and their small enterprises are responsible for almost all the economic growth in the United States."[31]

Members of Congress were eager to stimulate the kind of entrepreneurial developments that were happening in the computing industry. For example, the Democratic senator Birch Bayh and the Republican senator Bob Dole collaborated on writing the well-known Bayh-Dole Act (passed in 1980), which effectively allowed universities and university researchers to capitalize financially on their research, even if it had been funded by the federal government. This provided incentives for universities to commercialize the results of their research and to focus their research much more on what could be commercialized. The research university emerged as a powerhouse of knowledge creation. Although industrial research remains important, university research has exploded. The university became the source of new knowledge to be transferred to the private sector.

In the subsequent period, from the early 1980s onward, the number of licenses issued by universities and the number of start-ups began to increase, due in part to the Bayh-Dole Act but also to other reforms and structural changes.[32] The Small Business Innovation Development Act of 1982 earmarked 1.25 percent of federal R&D funds for small companies. This program funded small high-tech companies over the decades and made technology available for commercial purposes.

Also in the late 1970s, reforms were made that permitted pension funds to invest in private equity, giving rise to institutionalized venture capital. This helped unleash the growth of a new form of entrepreneurial finance. Between 1946 and 1977, the creation of new venture funds amounted to less than a few hundred million dollars annually. Starting in the late 1970s and culminating in the late 1990s, fundraising in the venture capital industry increased sharply. Although most of this money went to IPOs and new business start-ups, some of it was used to fund industrial innovation. It is estimated that venture capital accounted for 8 percent of industrial innovations from 1983 to 1992, and 14 percent by 1998.[33]

Much of the entrepreneurial investment in America's information infrastructure was made during the 1980s. For example, Michael Milken, who would later achieve notoriety for his involvement in insider trading, invested twenty-one billion dollars in the information industry. His largest commitments were to MCI, Tele-Communications Inc., McGraw Cellular Communications Inc., Turner Broadcasting, Time Warner Inc., and Metromedia Broadcasting. Virtually devoid of conventional collateral, none of these companies could have raised comparable sums from other sources. The original investment of ten billion dollars in these companies had a market value of sixty-two billion dollars in 1993. This web of glass and light is today an essential resource for America's information economy.[34]

## The Entrepreneurial Economy

Before going further, it's important to understand what this increasingly entrepreneurial society looks like. Five distinct features are noteworthy:

- *Markets and individual firms are replacing bureaucracies.* As Norman Macrae suggests, bureaucratic production cannot work because managers will not introduce labor-saving technologies.[35] The implicit compact between "big labor, big business, and big government" that once existed in the managed economy has disappeared. Labor's share of the workforce has fallen dramatically, big business is in flux,[36] and government functions are increasingly being contracted out to the private sector.

- *Knowledge is more important than physical capital.* Knowledge and the universities that produce new knowledge are far more important now than they were in the early twentieth century. Today, the university is an integral part of the institutional infrastructure of the entrepreneurial society, where knowledge has replaced brawn as the most important input into production. As suggested by *The Economist*, the "Knowledge Factory" (the university) has become the most important institution in generating knowledge to fuel the entrepreneurial society.[37]

- *Firm structure is more dynamic.* After World War II, large firms dominated the U.S. economy, often in oligopolies. Turnover among these firms was minimal and new firms played a minor role. This has changed dramatically in the past several decades. New firms offering new products and services (in IT, biotechnology, and retail) and foreign entrants into traditional industries (such as automobiles and steel) have been major drivers, if not *the* main driver, of economic growth. Hallmarks of entrepreneurial firms are relatively flat management structures and rapid responsiveness to market demands, whereas large firms typically feature more bureaucratic, hierarchal management and slower decision making. This is consistent with both the observation of Norman Macrae that educated people do not want to be organized top down and Peter Drucker's point that organizations are more like tents than pyramids.

- *The nature and process of innovation are very different.* Led by risk-taking entrepreneurs, new firms are disproportionately responsible for "radical" or "breakthrough" technologies, although larger managerial firms are typically needed to refine, mass produce, and market these technologies. The innovations that now characterize modern life—the automobile, telephone, airplane, air conditioning, personal computer, most software, and Internet search engines—were all developed and commercialized by entrepreneurs. Radical innovations tend to generate faster overall growth than incremental improvements. For example, the IT revolution, which was ignited largely by entrepreneurial companies, has statistically accounted for the significant acceleration in U.S. productivity growth over the past decade.

- *Equal opportunity for all.* In the managed economy, government closed the model. In other words, government was the recipient of residual income through income and inheritance taxes. In an entrepreneurial society, by contrast, one can get rich! The final arbiter of wealth reconstitution is the third sector—philanthropy. This uniquely American mechanism allows society to sustain itself without institutionalizing existing class structures.

## Why Did the Information Revolution Happen in America?

The question has no easy answer, as tempting as it might be to credit technology or luck and hard work. As I've discussed, the information revolution is particularly puzzling because it emerged out of an economy—and a sector—that had, on the whole, grown rigid and bureaucratic. Or at least that's how it appeared. Others like Gates and Allen must have seen the economy very differently. In his memoir, Paul Allen recalls reading *Fortune* magazine with Bill Gates, who told him in the late 1960s that he aspired to run his own company one day. Later, in the 1970s, when Gates and Allen had decided to go into the software business together, the idea that they could become rich together had not faded.

Allen recounts the effort they devoted to writing their first programming language: "We were building the first native high-level programming language for a microprocessor. Occasionally we wondered if some group at M.I.T. or Stanford might beat us, but we'd quickly regain focus. Could we pull it off? . . . . We had the energy and the skill, and we were hell-bent on seizing the opportunity. . . . We worked till all hours, with double shifts on weekends. Bill basically stopped going to class. . . . I neglected my job at Honeywell, dragging into the office at noon. I'd stay until 5:30, and then it was back . . . until three or so in the morning."[38] This prodigious effort was taking place in 1973, a time when IBM ruled computing and the American economy could not have been more managerial. Yet, undercurrents of this technological revolution were under way, and its proponents had enough faith that they would be able to cash in on their product if it indeed worked.

Allen continues, describing Bill Gates's drive: "I'd occasionally catch Bill grabbing naps at his terminal during our late-nighters. He'd be in the middle of a line of code when he'd gradually tilt forward until his nose touched the keyboard. After dozing for an hour or two, he'd open his eyes, squint at the screen, blink twice, and resume precisely where he'd left off—a prodigious feat of concentration."[39] Although the American economy seemed destined in the 1970s to be run by the perennial giants of industry, there existed an underlying can-do culture and belief in American entrepreneurship that would usher in a new era of cowboy capitalism.

This is not the answer we are looking for, however. The reason the information technology revolution happened in America is in part the story of Gates and Allen, but it is also the story of American exceptionalism. America allows, encourages, and funds radical innovations that bring about change. Radical innovation, as opposed to incremental innovation, involves the creation of new products that will displace old ones. The automobile industry displaced the coach industry, the personal computer displaced both the mainframe and the mechanical typewriter, the electronic cash register displaced the mechanical cash register, electric lighting displaced gas lighting, and cell phones are displacing land lines.

Incremental innovation—a new bumper on a car, a better handle on a kitchen appliance, a better-designed light—do not require eliminating existing industries, laying off workers, or making someone rich. In fact, many of the more managed economies in the world, such as Germany and Japan, focus on incremental, not radical, innovation and close collaboration among business, labor, and government as the sources of their comparative advantage.

Radical innovation, a form of creative destruction, has two outcomes. First, radical innovation allows for the displacement of old industries. For most of the twentieth century, Dayton, Ohio, was the home of the National Cash Register Company. The company got rich as it sold its machines all over the world, and it rewarded its workers with high wages and benefits and its hometown with firm civic guidance. Dayton's dominance in cash registers and numerous other industrial innovations did not last forever, however.[40]

The information revolution led to a shift in the knowledge base, and the mechanical cash register was replaced with optical scanners and computers in virtually every retail establishment. The invention of the microprocessor, the scanner, the bar code, and the PC allowed the replacement of the mechanical cash register at the checkout counter. After a hostile takeover of National Cash Register by ATT in 1991, the financially strapped company was downsized and finally spun off.[41] Dayton never recovered its former glory. Most of the workers at National Cash Register lost their jobs and could not find work in new industries: they could not write computer code. This technological shift destroyed existing opportunity for workers, firms, and communities. Radical innovations displace workers, leading to unemployment and destroying some opportunity while creating other opportunity, as discussed in chapter 2.

Second, radical innovations reward the entrepreneurs who bring them to market. This is the way American-style capitalism is set up. Gates and Allen became very rich because the software they wrote was incorporated into almost every PC sold, first in the United States and later around the world. They and countless others innovated and became rich. The next chapter examines the issue of wealth.

## Conclusion

As I discussed earlier, the return to entrepreneurial capitalism and the creation of new innovative firms spanned a number of industries, including steel, which had long been dominated by perennial giants. Furthermore, politicians and government programs actively supported these changes in the economy; they were helping the United

States compete against economies, such as Germany's and Japan's, that were reemerging after their postwar eclipse, as well as creating jobs and generally moving the economy forward. Today, economists tend to agree that technological innovation, like that created by firms like Microsoft, is responsible for about 50 to 75 percent of the growth in the U.S. economy since the postwar period.

It seems likely that policymakers will continue to be bullish on promoting radical innovations. Nonetheless, these changes in the economy have no doubt contributed to the growing income disparities in America over the past thirty years. As during the first Gilded Age, the great entrepreneurs concentrated wealth in the hands of a small number of people.

In part because of side effects such as increasing economic inequality, it is tempting to grow nostalgic when thinking about the period of the managed economy. The 1950s were, after all, a good time for the American economy. For white-collar workers, employment was steady and predictable. For blue-collar workers, union jobs in factories were higher paying and less prone to disappearing overseas or being displaced by technological advancements. In terms of innovation, the managed economy also seemed attractive, with the great corporate research laboratories like Xerox PARC and Bell Labs, which brought together some of the finest minds in science and engineering. Yet, all this stability and predictability was made possible by the limited nature of competition in the economy. Companies such as Xerox and IBM had almost no competition in the United States or globally for the products they sold and the services they provided.

The United States may return to the managed economy one day, but this seems very unlikely. Businesses are forced to remain trim and agile to compete globally and policy-makers know, or should know, that they need to stoke the engines of innovation in order to move the economy forward. Schumpeter and his contemporaries were wrong about the future of capitalist society. They erred in under-estimating the deep-rooted nature of creative destruction in the American economy. The entrepreneurial spirit would reemerge from America's past and rise to challenge bureau-cratic hegemony.

# CHAPTER 4

# THE WEALTH OF NATIONS

What is most important for democracy is not
that great fortunes should not exist, but that great
fortunes should not remain in the same hands.

—ALEXIS DE TOCQUEVILLE

## The Golden Spike

Since the beginning of the twentieth century, the American research university has increasingly moved to the forefront of innovation, playing a more critical role in developing new technologies used by large companies and entrepreneurs. In recent decades, one university and one region in particular have become almost synonymous with knowledge creation and the high-tech industry: Stanford University and Silicon Valley. The university plays an integral part in the success of its region, in part because many of its alumni work in nearby technology companies but also because many of the inventions created at Stanford, particularly by faculty and graduate students, are commercialized and turned into businesses that become part of Silicon Valley's high-tech economy.

Today, Stanford University is extraordinarily successful. It has a sixteen-billion-dollar endowment, enrolls roughly fifteen thousand students, and is ranked top in many fields, including engineering and technology, life and physical sciences, and health sciences.[1] Silicon Valley is also stunningly successful. It is home to thirty-three of the hundred largest high-tech firms launched since 1965, including Apple, Google, Netflix, Oracle, Sun Microsystems, Cisco Systems, Intel, National Semiconductor, Excite, and Yahoo. Silicon Valley also has one of the highest percentages of high-tech firms with fewer than twenty employees (55.9 percent) and one of the highest percentages of locally owned high-tech firms (65.9 percent).[2]

The strength of Stanford University today as both a center of innovative research and a leader in higher education is due to many factors, including the considerable amount of grant money the federal government has awarded to Stanford professors and graduate students. Stanford has also been sustained by a history of private giving that dates back to its founding by a railroad tycoon. Indeed, Stanford today is as interconnected with the gears of American capitalism as it was at its founding. Although Leland Stanford may not have imagined the heights to which his university would reach, he aimed to "qualify students for personal success and direct usefulness in life," no doubt to perpetuate the middle-class values that had shaped his own life.

By the time he donated his fortune to create a university in the name of his dead son, Leland Stanford was a businessman and former governor. He had migrated to California during the Gold Rush in the early 1850s and then made a number of lucrative investments in the railway business. Then, from self-interested behavior in business he turned to focusing on new ways to put his fortune to use. The year after the death of their only child, Stanford and his wife gave the money to create a university named in honor of their late fifteen-year-old son, commenting that now "the children of California shall be our children."

Leland was born in 1824 into a family of eight children of Josiah and Elizabeth Stanford. His father was a farmer, and they lived on the family farm in central New York state. Leland attended a local school until 1836, after which he attended the Liberal Institute in Clinton, New York. He studied law at Cazenovia Seminary in Cazenovia, New York, from 1841 to 1845. After graduating, he went to work in the law offices of Wheaton, Doolittle & Hadley in Albany. He was admitted to the bar in 1848 and subsequently moved to Port Washington, Wisconsin, where he practiced law with Wesley Pierce, and then to California in 1852.

During this time, America was still being stitched together by the railroad. Leland Stanford was president of the Central Pacific Railroad, in which he and three other prominent businessmen were the key investors, and he focused his efforts on building the railroad over the Sierra Nevada Mountains. In 1868 he formed the Pacific Union Express Company, which laid the track from the west that connected to the transcontinental railroad being built from the east. On May 10, 1869, in Promontory, Utah, Leland Stanford hammered in the famous golden spike to signal the completion of one of history's great engineering feats, the meeting of the two segments of the transcontinental railroad. His most enduring legacy was yet to come, however.

In creating Stanford University, Leland's vision was to provide a "practical education," a vision that still guides the university more than one hundred years later. Stanford had wanted to create a university that was nontraditional: a coeducational, nondenominational institution that was avowedly practical and would produce "cultured and useful citizens." In the fall of 1885, Stanford dedicated the founding grant for Stanford University at his country house. The document was accepted by the twenty-four members of the university's first board of trustees on November 14 in San Francisco. It defined the scope, responsibility, and organization of the university and defined its mission: "To qualify students for personal success and direct usefulness in life; and to promote the public welfare by exercising an influence on behalf of humanity and civilization, teaching the blessings of liberty regulated by law, and inculcating love and reverence for the great principles of government as derived from the inalienable rights of man to life, liberty, and the pursuit of happiness."[3]

The value of that practical education has been validated in the university's research laboratories. The university has been a leader in technology transfer for a decade, and its labs have produced inventions that are now used by millions of people around the world: computers, cell phones, search engines, and so on. When Google went public, Stanford University received millions from its founders, Sergey Brin and Larry Page, who attended Stanford's doctoral program in computer science before dropping out to found the company in a rented garage.

The university's initial endowment was considerable and included eight thousand acres on which to build the university. In 1898, after the death of her husband, Jane Stanford sold her railroad holdings and turned over eleven million dollars to the university trustees, along with some of the original buildings. A century later, Stanford now has a research budget of $806 million, second only to Johns Hopkins University, and an operating budget of more than $1.5 billion.

Stanford University has grown considerably since the Stanfords' initial contributions, and philanthropic contributions have sustained the university's ability to compete as one of the best in the world. In 2002, annual giving to the university totaled more than $450 million, second only to Harvard University. Total giving was 26 percent from alumni, 4 percent from parents, 40 percent from other individuals, 18 percent from foundations, 7 percent from corporations, and 5 percent from other sources. Between 1993 and 2002, donations to Stanford increased by 150 percent. Today, Stanford's endowment is 63 percent greater than that of the whole University of California system, with its ten campuses.[4]

Perhaps no university can claim to have had a greater economic impact in the last quarter of the twentieth century than Stanford. It has built a community of scholars and a world-class network of alumni, and its graduates have founded many of the most successful high-tech companies in the world, including Hewlett-Packard (William Hewlett and David Packard), Cisco Systems (Leonard Bosack and Sandra Lerner), and Google (Sergey Brin and Larry Page).

## The Problem of Wealth

The defining feature of capitalism, whether American or some other style, is not greed or the social ills that have long caused great misery, oppression, war, famine, and devastation. Capitalists have been and are still greedy. But the defining characteristic of capitalism has been its amazing wealth-generating capacity. The power of that wealth transformed traditional societies and continues to allow human societies to do remarkable things.[5]

Underlying the history of Stanford University and its benefactor is a story about wealth. But it is not a story of idle wealth or necessarily of privileged wealth, but rather of wealth that was earned by Leland Stanford, a lawyer turned railroad entrepreneur, and used to generate more wealth through "qualifying students for personal success and direct usefulness in life." Stanford did not hoard his money but instead used it to create opportunities for others who had the ambition, as he had, to work hard and make something of themselves.

The Stanford story seems free of the stereotypical behavior of the wealthy, with an aristocratic class holding on to its vast inheritance and using it either to enjoy lives of leisure or to erect institutions to protect its holdings. Of course, wanting to preserve what one has earned is a natural inclination, which is why nobody really *wants* to pay taxes, even when they believe that doing so is ultimately useful for society. It is worth asking, however, how much money one actually needs to preserve. As the eminent economist John Maynard Keynes pointed out in his famous 1930 essay "Economic Possibilities for Our Grandchildren," "The love of money as a possession . . . will be recognized for what it is, a somewhat disgusting morbidity, one of those semi-criminal, semi-pathological propensities which one hands over with a shudder to the specialists in mental disease."[6]

In this book, it should be clear that I'm very bullish on the need for entrepreneurship and innovation. I've spent my entire academic career studying how important these forces are for economic growth. One externality of these forces, however, is that successful entrepreneurship can concentrate wealth, as it did in the late nineteenth century, when Leland Stanford was building railroads, and is doing again today. Since the 1970s, around the time the entrepreneurial economy I described in chapter 3 took hold, the median income growth in the United States has been relatively flat. Nonetheless, huge amounts of wealth have been created. For instance, the Dow was at 600 in 1970. By the 2000s, the Dow was above 10,000. Between 1980 and 2000, median household net worth increased from $130,000 to $400,000, in 2001 dollars. This kind of wealth creation was entirely unprecedented in the immediate postwar decades.

Looking back on the 1950s and 1960s, it is clear that an attractive feature of the managed economy of mid-twentieth-century America was that it was stable and predictable. Sure, there were rich people and poor people, but there were few opportunities for individuals to become megarich because the system resisted change—it resisted introducing radically new products and innovations that would upset the status quo. There were few major innovations and almost no entry of new firms into existing industries. For individuals, there was opportunity in the sense that men could work hard and work their way up in a company. This was not going to radically change the structure of the economy or how business was done, however—all of this was largely established in the routine relationships among business, labor, and government.

In an entrepreneurial society, by contrast, there is wealth creation—and lots of it. Indeed, a fundamental outcome of successful entrepreneurship is the accumulation of money. Over the centuries, wave after wave of entrepreneurs have exploited opportunities and created great wealth. In the eighteenth century, it was the merchant traders and planters; in the nineteenth century, it was the industrialists and financiers; and in the twentieth century, it was the great innovators in technology and manufacturing, automobiles, planes, and electronics. With these innovations came jobs and economic opportunities for millions of Americans, as well as improved living standards and cheaper, more abundant goods and services.

Most recently, the information revolution has brought innovations in computers, mobile telephones, the Internet, and information and communication technologies. Key innovators include Bill Gates in software, Gordon Moore in microprocessors, and Larry Page and Sergey Brin in search engines. Large amounts of wealth were also created in finance (George Soros), biotechnology (Robert Swanson), and entertainment (Oprah Winfrey). With these innovators, the number of billionaires has increased from 13 in 1982 to 400 in 2010; the number of decamillionaires stands at 250,000, and millionaires at 5.1 million in 2010. So much wealth has been created that commentators have suggested that we've entered a second Gilded Age. In the mid-twentieth century, 80 percent of those on the *Forbes* list of the richest Americans had inherited their money. Today, that portion has fallen to less than 10 percent.

## Income Inequality, the Great Divergence

As the wealth associated with new entrepreneurial innovations has been concentrated at the upper end of the income distribution, the overall picture of income inequality—the ratio of wealth for the richest Americans compared to the poorest Americans—has started to look more like that of a developing country. As Thomas Noah wrote in *Slate* magazine at the end of a ten-part series on income inequality, "I find myself returning to the gut-level feeling expressed at the start of this series: I do not wish to live in a banana republic. There is a reason why, in years past, Americans scorned societies starkly divided into the privileged and the destitute. They were repellent. Is it my imagination, or do we hear less criticism of such societies today in the United States? Might it be harder for Americans to sustain in such discussions the necessary sense of moral superiority?"[7]

Income inequality presents a moral dilemma for society when it deprives citizens of opportunity. Although the hoarding of wealth at the top end of the distribution would probably not move society back to the stark paradigm of lords and peasants, some of the undesirable qualities of limited economic opportunity would emerge. Such a system slows down the forces of creative destruction and causes the machinery of opportunity to seize up for the rest of society. It would also have long-term effects on the purchasing power of most Americans, challenging their ability to afford the goods and services that make the economy strong.

The severity of income inequality in the United States has had ups and downs over the past century. Figure 1 shows the income share of the top 10 percent of income earners over the past ninety years. Let's break this picture down into three periods: from 1917 to 1930 is the end of the first Gilded Age; from 1930 to 1979 is the period of the managed economy; and the period from 1980 to the present is the emergence of a new Gilded Age. In general, the gilded ages are associated with periods of high inequality, whereas the managed economy—which included national initiatives such as the New Deal and the Great Society, along with higher taxes on the wealthy—is associated with lower income inequality.

Because of successful entrepreneurship's ability to generate huge amounts of wealth, it should be associated with lots of income inequality. If we get in the way of entrepreneurship, there will be less income inequality, but there will also be less innovation, which could lead to deeper problems in

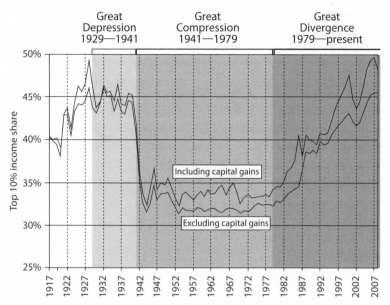

| Great Depression 1929—1941 | Great Compression 1941—1979 | Great Divergence 1979—present |

**Figure 1.** The Top 10 Percent Income Share, 1917–2008
*Note:* Income is defined as market income (and excludes government transfers). In 2008, the top decile includes all households with annual income greater than $109,000.
*Source:* Thomas Piketty and Emmanuel Saez, http://rwer.wordpress.com/2010/09/20/graph-of-the-week-the-top-10-income-share-in-usa-1917-2008/.

a globally competitive economy. The entrepreneurial revolution of the 1980s and the 1990s pretty well explains the rise in the share of income of the top 10 percent—as well as the rise of the top 1 percent (see figures 2a and 2b). Entrepreneurs made lots of money investing in the inventions of the information and communications technology revolution and starting companies.

In addition to the billions that have accrued to entrepreneurs, many others have taken advantage of the increasing returns to education, mostly at the top ends of the income distribution. As more and more students went to college and graduate school, increasing their human capital, the

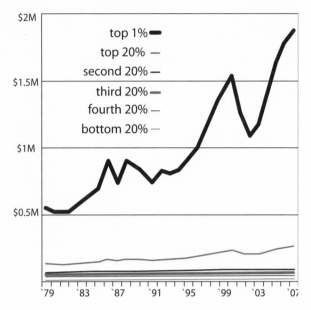

**Figure 2a**. Average Household Income before Taxes (2007 dollars)
*Source:* Congressional Budget Office.

income gaps between high school education, college education, and graduate-level education increased. During the managed economy, however, much of the industrial technology favored mass production and semiskilled labor, so skilled workers were relatively much better off compared to college-educated workers, even if the skilled worker's only academic credential was a high school diploma.

## What to Do with Wealth

What to do with wealth is an age-old dilemma. For societies, the puzzle is figuring out the right allocation among three basic options: wealth can be kept in the family, taxed by the government, or given away. Many societies have

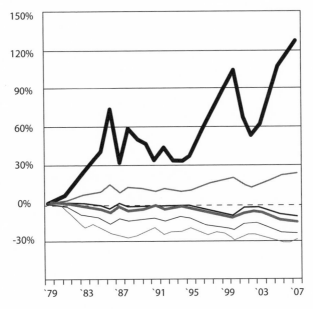

**Figure 2b**. Change in Share of Income vs. 1979, after Taxes
*Source:* Congressional Budget Office.

encouraged different combinations of these options, and the United States is no exception. Nonetheless, Americans, for reasons I will discuss in this chapter and the next, have made innovations regarding exactly how money should be given away and what sorts of institutions it should be used to support. This creativity began with early Americans such as Peter Faneuil and Benjamin Franklin and continued over the centuries with others like George Peabody, Leland Stanford, and Bill Gates. The American tradition has welcomed entrepreneurial activity and encouraged vast amounts of wealth creation, but it has tended to avoid the establishment of a ruling class. In other words, American institutions have been built around creating opportunity for middle-class people to get rich, and also ensuring that wealth be recycled *outside* of the family.

In class-based societies, "wealth" is not a problem; the class system necessitates that there be wealthy people. In Europe for much of modern history, the wealthy had money because they were from the nobility and they were the nobility because they were wealthy. In an entrepreneurial society, by contrast, people are wealthy because they have worked hard and seized opportunity. Their children may have money as well, but if the incentives and value system are in a healthy equilibrium, capitalism creates more great institutions like Stanford University and fewer idle, self-indulgent heiresses. As Herbert and Marion Sandler, the billionaire former co-CEOs of Golden West Financial, put it, "How many residences, automobiles, airplanes and other luxury items can one acquire and use?"[8]

## Philanthropy, an American Invention

Philanthropy has helped address America's problem of wealth by serving two basic functions. It releases the concentration of wealth at the top of society while building institutions that support opportunity for future Americans. Philanthropists are typically entrepreneurs and, as such, they tend to value institutions that promote and facilitate entrepreneurial activity—that is, institutions that reward hard work, ambition, and innovation, like the modern American university.

In America, those who make their fortunes rather than inherit them are more likely to be philanthropists. A 2006 survey of high-net-worth households conducted by Indiana University's Center on Philanthropy found that entrepreneurs who earned at least half their fortunes by starting businesses are the most generous with their money, contributing twice as much as those who gained their fortunes through inheritance.[9] As Thomas J. Tierney writes in *Philanthropy* magazine, "Business is the engine of our society's wealth. . . . Not surprisingly, businesspeople-turned-philanthropists often want to apply a similar sort of analytical thinking to their gift-giving."[10]

Credit for the American invention of philanthropy should be given to the influential and successful Baltimore investor George Peabody, a descendent of Massachusetts Puritans who was born in 1795. Despite the mark he made on finance in Baltimore, Peabody's most enduring influence lies in the precedents and policies established by the Peabody Education Fund trustees. This fund innovated the operational patterns of later major foundations, including John D. Rockefeller's Education Board, the Russell Sage Foundation, and the Carnegie Foundation. According to Peabody's biographer, Franklin Parker, "George Peabody was in fact the originator of that system of endowed foundations for public purposes which has reached its highest development in the United States. . . . . It is interesting to consider the many ways in which the example set by [George Peabody] has been followed by visioned men of means in the United States. . . . . In a sense the Peabody Fund was not the only monument to George Peabody, for the example he set has been followed by a host of other Americans."[11] Indeed, many aspects of philanthropy have been bound to the capitalist system, including the fortunes of those who have created philanthropic institutions, as well as their values and approach to pathbreaking methods of mobilizing wealth, such as the foundation.

Many philanthropists have even taken the language of business and applied it to their giving. Today, Ely and Edythe Broad talk about their approach to giving as "venture philanthropy." These philanthropists have retired from the business that made them billionaires and have devoted themselves full-time to their grantmaking activities. They write, "We view our grants as investments, and we expect a return—in the form of improved student achievement for our education reform work, treatments or cures for disease in our scientific and medical research, and increased access to the arts."[12]

Similarly, Jeff Skoll, a cofounder of eBay, has made investments in social entrepreneurship (one form of the type of venture philanthropy that Ely and Edythe Broad practice), seeking innovative ways to solve social problems, much like KaBOOM! (discussed in chapter 2). Skoll grew up in a middle-class family in Canada. Early in life, his dream was to be a writer whose stories would make a difference in the world. Nonetheless, he went to business school and became the first president of eBay. When the company went public, he became a multimillionaire. The first thing he did was to start the Skoll Foundation, which has become the leading organization supporting social entrepreneurship.[13]

The other cofounder of eBay, Pierre Omidyar, has pursued a similar path. He and his wife, Pam, write, "We invest in for profit businesses that serve overlooked populations with much-needed products and services. We reach out to like-minded investors and advocates to form coalitions that support issues that will benefit from a unified voice."[14] Thus, the Omidyars are literally using money from their entrepreneurial activities to generate more business development, but focusing on serving populations that the market has, for whatever reason, overlooked. The Broads, Jeff Skoll, and the Omidyars have all committed to giving away more than half of their fortunes to such philanthropic ventures.

I started this chapter discussing wealth and how huge disparities in wealth could lead to a society in which an elite has disproportionate power and influence. In some ways, philanthropy might not seem to alleviate this problem: even though the money is spent on ventures that create opportunity, the power of the purse is still in the hands of the wealthy. It has been difficult for philanthropists to act when there is not already a groundswell of demand, or a reform movement under way that is aligned with their goals.

In the late nineteenth century, Andrew Carnegie was devoted to using his wealth to support institutions that would lead to the development of "learned" society. Two of his favorites were universities and libraries, but local democratic forces sometimes preferred to spend money in other ways. In eastern Pennsylvania, in the region where his steel business had flourished, Carnegie proposed to build a library in any town that would put up 10 percent of the cost. Ultimately, twenty of the forty-six towns voted against the offer.[15] Perhaps the labor unions, which were the dominant democratic forces in these regions, saw little benefit from having libraries. Or perhaps they were resentful of the way Carnegie ran his business. Historically, some of the major projects supported by philanthropists have arguably been counterdemocratic—opposed in localities by popular movements, as charter schools sometimes are today. In this sense, philanthropy appears dictatorial, manipulated from above by the puppet strings of successful industrialists.

Consider Carl C. Icahn, the legendary Wall Street raider, who described his approach as buying undervalued companies that often were poorly managed and creating shareholder value through better management. His approach to education reform certainly resembles the ambitions of a shakeup artist. In his Giving Pledge statement he refers to children from underprivileged backgrounds as "undervalued assets." He goes on to describe how his foundation invests in vocational schools for such students because he believes that "without significantly changing the method we use to educate our young students in this country, [America] will soon lose [its] hegemony."[16] Philanthropy appeals to those who want to push the boundaries and to experiment with innovative approaches to solving old problems.

Philanthropy, like the entrepreneurial economy I described in chapter 3, is unmanaged—it does not emanate from a set of government programs nor is it constrained in obvious ways by some "triangle" relationship among labor, business, and government, as John Kenneth Galbraith described American society at midcentury. For these very reasons, however, philanthropy is sometimes viewed with suspicion. Although some suspicion is warranted, it is worth noting that philanthropy, while unmanaged, is bound by other partnerships. The development of philanthropic initiatives could not have been carried out by actors like Carl Icahn and John D. Rockefeller alone. Rather, philanthropy has always been constrained by a partnership between the rich who made their own fortunes and various progressive elites of academia, local government, the judiciary, and other professional organizations. Together these interests figured out how to put the new money to work for privately funded public goods: education, science, public health, and knowledge creation.

The University of Chicago offers an interesting example. In a way, the founding of the university was a partnership between the oil magnate John D. Rockefeller and the child prodigy William Rainey Harper, who by the age of nineteen had finished his PhD at Yale, where his dissertation compared prepositions in Latin, Greek, Sanskrit, and Gothic.[17] In addition to being brilliant, Harper also possessed a shrewd business acumen and when Rockefeller appointed him president of the University of Chicago, he devoted himself to transforming it into a modern research university. The partnership between Harper and Rockefeller was between an oil entrepreneur and an academic entrepreneur, both of whom were devoted to maximizing the excellence of the university. Chicago quickly moved in many new and innovative directions as Rockefeller continually put money into the university until his death forty years later and as Harper ceaselessly sought to move the university in new and innovative ways and to attract top academic talent. Thus philanthropy was married to a network of academic reforms.

As the goals of reformers evolve over time, so does philanthropy. As a driver of social change, philanthropy focuses on the social conditions underlying issues such as women's rights, gay rights, racial segregation, and so on. This form of philanthropy was prevalent in the second half of the twentieth century, driven by issues such as segregation and civil rights in the United States. Rather than focusing on individual problems, the agenda of social transformation focuses on the broader society.[18] Although the roots of this approach, especially that of Johns Hopkins, can be found in the abolitionist movements of the 1800s, it was only in the 1960s and later that it became the dominant paradigm for many foundations. Even though the paradigm shift was driven mostly by social issues, it has been sustained by the work of renowned entrepreneurs who built foundations to carry out social reforms and address the systemic causes of social ills.

## Charity and Philanthropy

While people like Franklin, Girard, and Peabody played an early role in forging a path for American philanthropy, Andrew Carnegie was the first to articulate philanthropy's place in society and to forcefully explain that this new way of giving money was different from what had gone before. Carnegie was self-educated, relying on access to public libraries, and he continued to educate himself throughout his life. Carnegie wrote extensively, including his most influential article, "Wealth," in which he presented his theory of philanthropy. Carnegie believed that people who had the ability to generate wealth had a duty to do so honestly and to amass the greatest fortune possible so they could use it to serve the public good. He saw becoming wealthy not as selfish but as a noble and virtuous act.[19]

Although charity and philanthropy often get conflated, in the context of this book it is important to emphasize their difference. Charity has been described as "generosity and helpfulness, especially toward the needy or suffering; aid given to those in need; an institution engaged in relief of the poor; [or] public provision for the relief of the needy."[20] Philanthropy in the Anglo-American tradition is not charity but a proactive or participatory action by an individual or organization whose mission is to enable those in need to help themselves. Lao Tzu's famous maxim helps to clarify the difference: charity is when you give a man a fish and feed him for a day, whereas philanthropy is when you teach a man to fish, enabling him to feed himself for a lifetime. Other distinctions provide further nuance.

Much confusion about giving stems from the failure to distinguish the philanthropic sector from the larger charitable sector. Although these two sectors interact with each other, their dissimilarities are important in any discussion of philanthropy. In the nineteenth century, reformers understood the distinction, as there was growing dissatisfaction with the efficacy of poorhouses and other institutions associated with charity.

Daniel Coit Gilman, the first president of Johns Hopkins University, explained the difference in his 1907 essay "Five Great Gifts." His argument was essentially that charity provided temporary relief for the needy. Philanthropy, by contrast, was for all humankind. It was to be national in scope and search for root causes. Rather than giving to cater to the needs of the poor and the needy, the focus of philanthropy was on "maximizing human potential" by creating and supporting institutions that will provide opportunities for both individual and civic improvement. Neighborhood societies, schools funds, civic projects, and civic clubs like the Junta created by Benjamin Franklin sprung from this paradigm. The goal of any philanthropic endeavor was to "develop useful civic improvements and practical solutions to social problems."[21]

Carnegie believed that philanthropy was the only "proper" way to dispose of wealth in a capitalist system, as it functions to help maintain the social order and provide direction for entrepreneurial efforts.[22] He believed that anyone could be successful if he or she had a good work ethic and was given the proper tools—a view that is still the folklore of the American Dream. Carnegie recognized that philanthropy is not charity or a way of helping the helpless but rather a way of giving a leg up to those who are willing to help themselves. In fact, Carnegie's views on charity were rather extreme. "It would be better to throw money into the sea than to give it to charity," he wrote.

Ely and Edythe Broad write, "We view charity and philanthropy as two very different endeavors. For many years, we practiced charity, simply writing checks to worthy causes and organizations."[23] For the Broads, philanthropy is about creating opportunity for individuals and getting results, thus implicitly challenging and improving the effectiveness of existing institutions.

Charity descends from a paternalistic society, in which giving by the wealthy is designed to demonstrate compassion for the poor in times of need. Charity is designed not to empower others but rather to sustain them—not necessarily in poverty, but not on a path to prosperity, either.

## The American Foundation

The Columbia University economist Jeffrey Sachs has articulated a position through which we can judge philanthropic activities based on past accomplishments. Creating opportunity for future generations is about creating knowledge today, and the model, according to Sachs, is the Rockefeller Foundation:

> The model to emulate is the Rockefeller Foundation, the preeminent development institution of the 20th century, which showed what grant aid targeted on knowledge could accomplish. Rockefeller funds supported the eradication of hookworm in the American South; the discovery of the Yellow Fever vaccine; the development of penicillin; the establishment of public-health schools (today's undisputed leaders in their

fields) all over the world; the establishment of medical facilities in all parts of the world; the creation and funding of great research centers such as the University of Chicago, the Brookings Institution, Rockefeller University, and the National Bureau of Economic Research; the control of malaria in Brazil; the founding of the research centers that accomplished the green revolution in Asia; and more.[24]

Having no precedent in other capitalist countries at the time, the American foundation had to be invented from scratch, which required organizational, technical, and legal innovation.[25] One of the lasting contributions of George Peabody, one of the greatest nineteenth-century philanthropists, was the creation of the foundation. He was a man of modest beginnings who gained a fortune through canny investment. He developed a philosophy of philanthropy that was dominated by two main considerations: a deep devotion to the communities in which he was reared and in which he made his money, and a secular vision of the Puritan doctrine of the stewardship of riches. His desire, in the simplest terms, was to be useful to humankind. In his lifetime, Peabody donated more than $130 million (in 2010 dollars) to libraries, science, housing, education, exploration, historical societies, hospitals, churches, and other charities.[26]

Peabody was interested in improving the human condition. By granting 3,645 Peabody scholarships for teacher training at Peabody Normal College in Baltimore from 1877 to 1904, his fund set a precedent in selecting, supporting, and channeling able, ambitious, and dedicated students, regardless of their income or status, into higher education. Peabody's commitment to education is illustrated in a letter he sent to his nephew in 1831: "Deprived, as I was, of the opportunity of obtaining anything more than the most common education, I am well qualified to estimate its value by the disadvantages I labor under in the society in which my business and situation in life frequently throws me, and willingly would I now give twenty times the expense attending a good education could I possess it, but it is now too late for me to learn and I can only do to those that come under my care, as I could have wished circumstances had permitted others to have done by me."[27]

The paradigm of improvement via philanthropy could also be traced to the industrial revolution, which benefited from the rationalization of work processes in factories.[28] Under this new paradigm, philanthropy also developed a management component; it was not just about giving but also about how resources were used and their impact. Skilled people became necessary to manage philanthropic institutions, which were gradually adopting scientific management methods that were the stepchildren of the industrial revolution.[29]

Bequeathing money after one's death was little better than charity in Carnegie's view. He asserted that if a person waits until he is dead to distribute his wealth, there is no guaranteeing it will do any good. He argued that it is most effective to use the same ability that generated wealth to give it away in ways most beneficial to society. Carnegie viewed estate taxes as a condemnation of the useless life of a wealthy person who did not give his money away while still living. In fact, he felt that it was a disgrace to die wealthy.[30]

Why was Carnegie so adamant that the wealthy not give their money away *after* they died? Carnegie believed that the wealthy had a duty to administer their money wisely and effectively to provide long-lasting benefits for the public good. He basically felt that they should use the same talent that helped them accumulate wealth to administer it.[31] This notion of *administering* wealth, instead of simply handing it over, defined the way in which the American foundation evolved.

Consider the Ford Foundation, which was giving away upward of fifty million dollars per year in the 1950s. According to the historian Olivier Zunz, "Henry [Ford] sought advice from one of the foundation's trustees, physicist and MIT president Karl Compton, on how to get 'the best thought available in the United States' so that he could 'most effectively and intelligently' put the foundation's enlarged resources to work for 'human welfare.'" In 1948, Ford picked Rowan Gaither, a promising program manager with experience at MIT and the Rand Corporation, to head a task force to create a program and policies for the foundation. In order to get innovative ideas working, Gaither brought together eleven men with experience in public policy and academia to lead the foundation. Some were friends from California and some from leading universities, including both physical and social scientists. The goal was nothing less than providing "each human being optimum spiritual and political freedom, opportunity, sense of responsibility, and happiness."[32]

The foundation was an American invention. American philanthropists pushed to have a legal framework so that their foundations would be protected in perpetuity. The goal was to have an organization, administered by experts, that could operate on a set of principles, without having to define specific projects. Trustees and officers establish guidelines, start new programs, and allocate grant dollars on their own authority, all with the goal of interpreting and serving the foundation's mission. The flexibility built into the American foundation has allowed philanthropic contributions bequeathed in one era to be used to tackle evolving problems in a later era.

Although the potential of the foundation to promote truly innovative work grew increasingly apparent during the twentieth century, the freedom of the foundation to operate without precise goals faced a series of challenges in the nineteenth century. Common law inherited from England prohibited the creation of open-ended trusts that would be administered from generation to generation by a board of trustees.

A colorful example involving the building of the New York City Public Library should make this clear. In 1884, Samuel Tilden wrote in his will that he wished for his fortune to be used to build a free public library in the city. Tilden had no children but had bequeathed generous sums to his nephews and nieces. Nonetheless, these relatives challenged the will to build the library on the grounds that it was not specific enough. The old laws of wills required a certain degree of specificity in the will, namely that the corporation to benefit already be established or that an actual entity be specified. Since the library in 1884 was merely an idea of Tilden, not a properly incorporated institution, Tilden's heirs were able to nullify the will in court and claim the entire fortune for themselves. The story did not end there, however. The New York City Public Library was indeed built with money from the Tilden Trust. After the court ruled in favor of the heirs, Tilden's longtime law partner Andrew Green worked to delay the distribution of the estate to Tilden's heirs. Using this delaying tactic as a bargaining chip, Green was able to persuade one of the heirs to give back part of the fortune. Thus, the Tilden Trust was used, in part, to help finance the construction of the library.

Following the Tilden affair, the New York state assembly passed the Tilden Act, which allowed for the legal recognition of bequests that were undefined, specifying only that a board of trustees be responsible for administering the trust. Thus, the Tilden affair and the later work of the New York assembly helped pave the way for the development of the American foundation, as well as establishing one of the most important libraries in America, with holdings that rival those of the Library of Congress and the libraries of Harvard and Yale universities.

After the Tilden Act was passed in New York, other states followed suit and passed similar laws to lay the groundwork for philanthropy. It thus became possible for individuals to bequeath their fortunes to the "well-being of mankind." In the later nineteenth century there were numerous court cases that helped shape the legal framework for the modern foundation. This framework was never legislated; instead, it grew out of numerous state and federal court cases in which heirs to fortunes challenged their parents' philanthropic generosity.

The foundation idea caught on. In 1915 there were twenty-seven foundations, and by 1930 there were two hundred. Today there are tens of thousands. The flexibility of this organizational structure has proven very popular in the United States. If you look only at grantmaking foundations, sixty foundations in the United States each have more than one billion dollars in assets—these are just private foundations, not corporate foundations like the Goldman Sachs Foundation or the General Motors Foundation. The largest private foundation is the Gates Foundation, with thirty-three billion dollars in assets; the Ford Foundation comes in second, with about eleven billion dollars in assets. The combined assets of the one hundred largest foundations in the United States total $232 billion.[33] If you look at the hundred largest foundations plus another 1,230 large U.S. foundations, the total amount of grants they make each year is roughly twenty billion dollars. Of this grant-making, $4.5 billion goes to health-related activities and a similar amount goes to education.

In 1891, John D. Rockefeller Sr. hired staff to help him manage his philanthropic endeavors. After the U.S. Congress refused to grant a charter for his philanthropic organization, Rockefeller successfully got the state of New York to charter the Rockefeller Foundation in 1913. This new form of philanthropic giving, motivated by Andrew Carnegie, John Rockefeller, and Margaret Olivia Sage, meant that philanthropy used a structure similar to the business corporation for its activities. This structure provided more flexibility than charitable trusts, the traditional mode of giving from English law, and boards of directors took responsibility for overseeing operations, differentiating their roles from those of trustees of charitable trusts.

Frederick T. Gates (1853–1929), an American Baptist clergyman and educator, was the principal business and philanthropic advisor to John D. Rockefeller from 1891 to 1923. By hiring Gates to advise him on his philanthropic endeavors, Rockefeller sent the message that philanthropy needed experienced and skilled technocrats, just as business needed competent managers, in order to move forward.

## Philanthropy and the University

It is impressive that nineteenth-century entrepreneurs had the foresight to devote their philanthropy to what would later become world-class American universities, which would fuel the information revolution at the end of the twentieth century. Ezra Cornell (who had made his fortune as an associate of Samuel Morse, the inventor of the telegraph), for example, donated land and much of his wealth to set up a land-grant college. In the case of Cornell University, the land-grant university became a marriage of the old-style university devoted to the liberal arts and scholarly research with a modern university devoted to practical research and learning. As discussed in chapter 2, in addition to Cornell, a number of today's eminent universities were founded in the last half of the nineteenth century with entrepreneurial money.

At the time that many of these philanthropists were considering using their fortunes to build new educational institutions, higher education in the United States was, to varying degrees, sectarian. Consider the histories of Harvard and Yale, not to mention Oxford and Cambridge in the United Kingdom. The marriage between capitalism and the university was only beginning. As the great industrialist and railroad entrepreneurs built their empires, they realized that to continue to grow, they would need professional managers and people with the most cutting-edge technical knowledge to drive industry forward. Their vision for education, therefore, emerged from their experiences with practical problems such as management, technology, and organization.

The earliest efforts to move schools toward offering more practical education started with Ben Franklin's College of Philadelphia (later called the University of Pennsylvania), which opened in 1751. Thomas Jefferson's University of Virginia, founded in 1819, hinted at the possibility of offering students more practical subjects, including sciences and math.[34] In his *Great American University*, Jonathan Cole writes: "In 1749, Benjamin Franklin outlined a course of education in a pamphlet entitled *Proposals for Education of Youth in Pennsylvania*. Students would be prepared for public service and business, quite a different mission from the ecclesiastical purposes outlined by Harvard and Yale. In keeping with Franklin's twin interests in science and in promoting useful knowledge, the University of Pennsylvania was designed to produce men of practical affairs rather than scholars or ministers. About one-third of the three-year curriculum was devoted to science and practical studies."[35] Philanthropists tended to create universities that promoted middle-class values. This differed from the mission of many other schools at the time, which had been set up under ecclesiastical auspices. A particularly noteworthy case is Johns Hopkins University, which was the first modern research university when it was established in 1876. Hopkins was founded when George Peabody—the same Peabody who set up the first American foundation—met with Johns Hopkins, a Baltimore merchant and financier. Peabody explained the basis of his philanthropy to Hopkins as using "the millions I have accumulated to accomplish the greatest good for humanity." Peabody's argument was convincing, and Hopkins responded by bequeathing seven million dollars—an extraordinary amount of money at that time—to found the Johns Hopkins University, Johns Hopkins Hospital, and several other related institutions.

Hopkins's history as a national research university began almost immediately as it was transformed into an American version of the German research university, focusing much more on research and graduate studies than any university in the United States had previously. Thus, Hopkins is another example of philanthropy challenging, in entrepreneurial ways, the system of education in the United States. Within four years of its founding, Hopkins, under the leadership of its president Daniel Coit Gilman, had twice as many graduate students as Harvard did and its faculty, astonishingly, had published almost twice as many research articles as the combined output of all other American universities.[36] In many ways, innovators like Gilman were adapting the German system of research education to an American university model.

Today, the investments that philanthropists made, and continue to make, in universities have created incredibly powerful incubators for entrepreneurial activity. Although government often provided the seed money, the universities produced the knowledge and educated the scientists and engineers. The university is only part of the later history of American capitalism. More broadly, the university keeps open the pathways of opportunity. When the western frontier was still unexplored, opening the path to opportunity was easily done without the university. Now, the university is a more integral part of opportunity—the American experiment has always kept opportunity open.

The university has not always been the driving force of American capitalism, although invention certainly has. Before the twentieth century, invention was generally easier in the sense that it did not necessarily require formal training—you needed an apprenticeship to a metalsmith, not a PhD in computer science. As the easier inventions, so the speak, are exploited, innovation must increasingly rely on knowledge-intensive breakthroughs, and capitalism therefore must rely on the university.

## Philanthropy Has Evolved over Time

A look at the philanthropic endeavors of a few of the wealthiest men in the knowledge economy shows that although they are a mixture of three traditions of philanthropy—focusing

on individuals, social institutions, and systemic change—
the strategy used stresses innovation, knowledge, and creativity at the level of both the individual and society. The
mottos and mission statements of the foundations these entrepreneurs created encapsulate this focus.

For example, the people-oriented Ellison Medical Foundation, which gets its money from Larry Ellison's Oracle
fortune, has focused on funding innovators in biomedical research. The Ellison Medical Foundation's founding
principles were that it would "fund people, not projects.
It would look for smart people who had track records of
creative, productive work and who had a good idea. Then it
would give them money and stand back." Thus the Ellison
Medical Foundation, in its own way, bypasses the traditional model of supporting institutions.[37]

Similarly, the Michael and Susan Dell Foundation has
pioneered a model for addressing educational challenges
by finding approaches that work and then helping to scale
them up. The foundation writes, "Once an effective and
pragmatic solution is identified, [the foundation] works
to facilitate replication of the solution. Underlying all the
foundation's efforts are a fundamental appreciation for
data and a belief that organizations that consistently measure and analyze results are those that offer the most effective and scalable solutions."[38]

The Internet and technology entrepreneurs Larry Page
and Sergey Brin used another innovative approach. From
the early stages of their company in 2004, they outlined a
commitment to contribute significant resources, including
1 percent of Google's equity and profits in some form, as
well as employee time, to address some of the world's most
urgent problems. That commitment became Google.org.
Google.org is an integral part of Google Inc., and it works

closely with a broad range of "Googlers" on projects that make the most of Google's strengths in technology and information. Google also established the Google Foundation 2005, which is a separate 501(c)(3) private foundation. The Google Foundation is managed by Google.org and supports its mission and core initiatives through grantmaking. Thus, this model is not limited to individuals, but can work through companies as well.

Although there are a lot of rich women in the United States today, few of them made their own fortunes. As we scan the landscape, one particular woman stands out. She was born in 1954 to a dirt-poor single mother in rural Mississippi, and for several years was raised by her grandmother on a pig farm. The woman in our story is, of course, Oprah Winfrey. More people in America know who Oprah is than who the president is. She was the first African American billionaire and the richest African American of the twentieth century. She has played major roles as a media mogul, an agent of social change, and a philanthropist.

Like Carnegie, Oprah enjoys making money for the pleasure of giving it away. Like Carnegie, she believes that success is earned, and gives away money to help people get started earning it. Like all the others in this chapter, Oprah is a firm believer that people must take responsibility for their lives and make an effort to help themselves. She doesn't have a long-term, systematic way of giving away her money, as Gates and Buffett do, and she is focused more on education and women's issues than on combating deeper social problems such as racial inequality and injustice.

Oprah has a philosophy of potential. She believes that each person has potential that is brought forth through education and experimentation, and self-transformation can help them reach their potential. In 2005, *Business Week* named her the greatest black philanthropist in American history. She gave away 13 percent of her net worth ($175 million) by 2005, and has given away 10 percent of her annual income since then, including five hundred thousand dollars to give children in Chicago an opportunity to get ahead. Like Peabody, Oprah is focused on self-empowerment and community-building, and, like George Soros, she has entered the international area.[39]

One might ask how individuals like Oprah get a shot at success—that is, at both ends of it: educational opportunity and entrepreneurial opportunity. Although there are many facets to this story, one stands out. The Ewing Marion Kauffman Foundation of Kansas City, Missouri, carries this vision forward in our society today. I was fortunate to be a senior fellow at the Kauffman Foundation and to experience firsthand the difference a foundation can make. The Kauffman Foundation has made entrepreneurship its mission: "To help individuals attain economic independence by advancing educational achievement and entrepreneurial success."[40] The story of Ewing Marion Kauffman, entrepreneur, civic leader, visionary, and philanthropist, is that of a great American who was also an ordinary person.[41]

Kauffman established the foundation with the same sense of opportunity he brought to his business endeavors and with the same convictions. He wanted his foundation to be innovative—to dig deep and get at the roots of issues to fundamentally change outcomes in people's lives—and to help young people, especially those from disadvantaged backgrounds, get a high-quality education that would enable them to reach their full potential. He saw building enterprise as one of the most effective ways to realize individual promise and spur the economy.[42]

## Conclusion

Capitalism is successful because it creates wealth, and most wealth generates economic opportunity through investments that seek to maximize private return. This is the gospel of the free market. The high levels of innovation and entrepreneurship in American capitalism have dramatically contributed to income inequality. By itself, income inequality is merely the natural consequence of a system that rewards hard work and innovation—qualities that don't appear to be evenly distributed in the population. Extremes of income inequality, however, could have many destabilizing features, particularly to the extent that concentrations of wealth work to close off economic opportunity to others.

This chapter began with Leland Stanford because he, along with his contemporaries, helped forge the relationship between creative destruction in the American economy and the institutions that promote opportunity. Thus, the economic openness that allowed entrepreneurs to accumulate fortunes has also nurtured social institutions, such as universities and foundations, that have in turn invested in and sustained future economic growth. This is the dynamic of American-style capitalism—*a self-sustaining cycle of wealth creation, social innovation, and opportunity that has endured over the centuries*. Therefore, the success of American-style capitalism—the standard by which Americans judge their society—must not rely on its transient ability to generate growth but on its sustained ability to generate opportunity.

Is this system of capitalism sustainable? How will the pressures of a new Gilded Age sustain or alter this system?

Despite the appeal of philanthropy—its obvious potential to recycle the wealth inherent in successful entrepreneurial societies—how sustainable is philanthropy as a system? On a basic level, it seems naïve to sit back and assume that America's billionaires will be moved by Carnegie's Gospel of Wealth or the letters of the Giving Pledge. These are not easy questions to answer. The next chapter traces the history of philanthropy and shows the extent to which it is woven into the very fabric of the American entrepreneurial experiment.

# CHAPTER 5

# CHARITY AND PHILANTHROPY

Give a man a fish and you feed him for a day.
Teach a man to fish and you feed him for a lifetime.

—LAO TZU

## Why We Give

Let's take a few minutes to ask a very simple question: Why are billionaires giving their money away? In order to understand philanthropy as a viable system for recycling wealth and creating opportunity, it's worth probing the dynamics that have sustained philanthropic giving and the conditions under which it has prospered and wavered.

In general, there is a considerable amount of generosity in the United States. Over the past few decades, the roughly three hundred fifty billion dollars given away each year amounts to roughly 2 to 3 percent of GDP. To put this in perspective, this amount is about equivalent to what the United States spends on research and development each year. Since reliable data has been collected, this aggregate figure has moved little more than a percentage point. Today, this would amount to each person in the United States giving about one thousand dollars on average. In a global perspective, the next most generous country is Britain, with about 1.5 percent of its GDP given away each year. There is no easy way to separate out what portion of this giving could be categorized as philanthropy, as opposed to charity.

Why is America, with its strong traditions of individualism and self-reliance, so generous? As I discuss in this chapter, this generosity goes back to the earliest Americans and seems to be rooted in their evolving cultural and religious traditions. To some extent, philanthropy has been sustained by bourgeois values, which have contributed to vast accumulations of wealth and shaped individual decisions about how wealth should be disbursed. Thus, the threads of philanthropic giving have been woven into the fabric of American capitalism. As Max Weber, the author of *The Protestant Ethic and the Spirit of Capitalism* and a devout proponent of capitalism, put it, "a man does not by nature wish to earn more and more money, but simply to live as he is accustomed to live and to earn as much as is necessary for that purpose."[1]

Like capitalism, philanthropy is not managed, at least not in obvious ways. As a result, there is considerable variation in terms of how much individuals actually give. Warren Buffett, Bill Gates, and Larry Ellison, the three wealthiest Americans according to the *Forbes* list, have all agreed to give away at least 95 percent of their wealth. By contrast, the Walton family, who are heirs to the fortune created by the deceased Sam Walton, the founder of Wal-Mart, have a combined wealth of about eighty billion dollars and a family philanthropic foundation with assets of about two billion dollars. Although two billion dollars is a terrific sum of money and has been used to pilot charter schools and support initiatives at the University of Missouri, it amounts to a small fraction of the family's overall wealth.

Sam Walton was able to transfer much of his wealth to his family using a device called a family limited partnership, thus circumventing much of the estate tax. Walton set up this partnership, Walton Enterprises, in 1953, in advance of making his fortune. This allowed him to give shares of Wal-Mart to his children. Thus, in 1992, when Sam Walton died, he owned only about 10 percent of the company because he had transferred the rest to his wife and children. The Walton heirs have not been known for their philanthropy, and they are not alone. Only about 20 percent of the billionaires in the United States have signed the Giving Pledge. Many of those who have not signed the pledge have made philanthropic contributions but have not committed themselves to giving away more than half of their wealth, as the pledge requires.

One predictor of philanthropy is whether the individual made his or her own money—a process that likely imbues one with a sense of the fragility of opportunity and the need to find ways to sustain it for others. Those who are self-made entrepreneurs, as opposed to having inherited their money, are far more generous on average. Indeed, much of the two billion dollars in the Walton Family Foundation came from Sam Walton himself, not from his children. If one looks globally at those individuals who have given away more than a billion dollars, only one of the nineteen inherited the money.[2] The linkage between entrepreneurial wealth creation and giving underpins part of what has made philanthropic giving so sustainable in the United States. The capitalist system has persistently injected new wealth into the system, ensuring that entrepreneurial values exist among those with wealth. Compare this to a system in which the wealthy have inherited all their money and thus have less personal connection to the value of opportunity.

Quite the opposite of middle-class values, however, are those of the aristocratic elite. Consider Ronald Lauder, heir to the fortune built through the entrepreneurial talents of his late mother, Estée Lauder, an Eastern European immigrant who started her career selling homemade beauty creams and eventually became the chairwoman of a company worth ten billion dollars, selling products in more than 130 countries. In 1960, she set up the Lauder Foundation and, with her husband, created the Joseph H. Lauder Institute of Management and International Studies at the University of Pennsylvania. Estée and Joseph Lauder's estate planning, including the use of family trusts like those used by the Waltons, allowed them to pass on nearly four billion dollars to their heirs, which was taxed at about 16 percent, roughly one-third of the top estate tax rate. As the *New York Times* writes, "As the son of a fabulously wealthy fashion icon, Mr. Lauder developed aristocratic tastes—and grand aspirations—at an early age. He summered in Vienna as a boy, developing a passion for Austrian art and medieval armor." Today, Lauder has an art collection valued at more than a billion dollars. He also has a philanthropic foundation, which has spent millions to help reestablish Jewish identity in Eastern Europe. His foundation is also used, however, as a way to establish tax exemptions for his art collection, predominately by loaning pieces to museums.[3]

## The Giving Pledge

Bill Gates was the richest man in the world when his mother convinced him to devote himself to philanthropy. Gates and his wife founded the Bill and Melinda Gates Foundation, the largest philanthropic foundation in the United States, which they endowed with twenty-two billion dollars. Their foundation is about four times as large, in constant dollars, as those of Carnegie and Rockefeller. The Gates Foundation's giving has included, among other grants, one hundred million dollars to fight childhood disease in developing countries and two hundred million dollars to buy computers for libraries.[4] The focus of the Gates Foundation, which will give away one billion dollars each year, includes education and health issues both in the United States and in the developing world. Warren Buffett merged his fortune into the Gates Foundation, which helped make it the largest philanthropic foundation in the world at thirty-two billion dollars.

The Giving Pledge, an idea put forth by Bill Gates and Warren Buffett, commits billionaires to give away one-half of their wealth in their lifetimes. In the summer of 2010, forty billionaires signed the pledge. As of mid-2012, a total of eighty-one billionaires have signed on.[5] The signatories of the Giving Pledge are almost all self-made billionaires, with the exception of Barron Hilton and David Rockefeller. That's seventy-nine entrepreneur-philanthropists to two inheritor-philanthropists. This is a huge commitment from a large number of billionaires; of the four hundred billionaires in the United States, approximately one-fifth have signed the Giving Pledge, and many of those who have not signed have individually given away billions.

Why do individuals give? In his so-called Gospel of Wealth, Andrew Carnegie wrote that the reason he gave his money away was because it was the duty of the man of wealth "to set an example of modest, unostentatious living, shunning display or extravagance; to provide moderately for the legitimate wants of those dependent upon him; and after doing so, to consider all surplus revenues which come to him simply as trust funds . . . . the man of wealth thus becoming the mere trustee and agent for his poorer brethren."[6] The letters that accompany the Giving Pledge represent a twenty-first-century Gospel of Wealth, giving a rare collective insight into the workings of and motivations behind American philanthropy. In order to understand why philanthropy is so strong in the United States, it is worth considering some of the attitudes revealed in the letters.

The motivations for giving all reflect overarching bour-geois, or middle-class, values, though three distinct themes emerge: wanting to make a difference in the lives of future generations; recognizing that luck and community play large roles in good fortune, and therefore wanting to give back; and feeling that enormous wealth should not be left to family.

None of the signatories directly invoke the promotion of social order as a reason for giving, as Carnegie did in his Gospel of Wealth. Rather, today's philanthropists usually speak, instead, of their duty to "give something back" to the society that helped make their own success possible. Why do rich people care about opportunity? Those with mod-est upbringings do because of their values. John and Laura Arnold, for example, who made a fortune trading natural gas via Enron, write, "We look upon our financial position with a mix of disbelief and humility, never having dreamed that we would be in this situation. Our backgrounds are similar to that of many Americans. We each had a solid middle-class upbringing with an emphasis on values, work ethic and social responsibility."[7] People with a middle-class background want to help others because that's how they were brought up.

Through the foundation model, most of those who have signed the Giving Pledge have devoted themselves to becoming stewards of their wealth. This idea is not new. Carnegie originated this vision in which money is not simply handed over to a church or another organization (which may not have the ability to manage it wisely), but instead carefully managed by the donor or the donor's foundation to ensure that it creates value. John D. Rockefeller III, for example, devoted himself full-time to managing the Rockefeller Foundation.

Today, this notion of managed stewardship plays a prominent role in philanthropy. Warren Buffett is fond of saying, "Making money is far easier than giving it away effectively." According to eBay cofounder Pierre Omidyar and his wife, "We don't just write checks, we engage deeply with the organizations we support."[8] These two work almost full-time on their philanthropic endeavors.

Similarly, the Giving Pledge signatories Eli and Edytha Broad, who were both raised in middle-class families, wrote, "About 10 years ago, we decided to focus full-time on philanthropy. We asked ourselves what was the greatest problem facing America. We both attended public schools and credit education as the foundation of our success. But we were dismayed by the state of America's K–12 public education system, and we wanted to work to restore it to greatness. We are convinced the future of the middle class, our standard of living, our economy and our very democracy rests on the strength of our public schools. And we have a long way to go."[9]

Many of the signatories have used the Giving Pledge to explain that they don't want their money to be used to create family dynasties. Herbert and Marion Sandler, who together built the savings and loan holding company Golden West Financial, amassed an entrepreneurial empire. Golden West was one of largest thrifts in the United States, with assets of approximately $125 billion, deposits of $60 billion, and twelve thousand employees before its 2006 acquisition by Wachovia.[10] Nonetheless, the Sandlers strongly opposed keeping in the family the tremendous wealth they had amassed. They wrote of their philanthropic pledge, "When you think about it, no other approach seems to make sense. Passing down fortunes from generation to generation can do irreparable harm."[11]

When the middle class first evolved, it was centered on economic mobility—the opportunity to use a skill or an idea to make money and improve one's life. In the rigid societies of the past, there was no mobile class. These values of mobility are brought out by many of the signatories, who reject the ideas of family dynasties and class societies. What they do believe in is equal opportunity: serving future generations to continue the adventure. They also often suggest that leaving money to children is not a good idea—that it is, in fact, a bad idea and inconsistent with American values. Looking after family is important, but too much is, well, too much. H. F. (Gerry) Lenfest made a fortune in publishing, communications, and cable television, and then sold his business to Comcast. Lenfest explained why he and his wife did not want to leave their fortune to their progeny: "Giving wealth to young and future unborn children, in our opinion, reduces or eliminates the character building challenges ahead of them in life that they would otherwise face."[12]

Harold Hamm is an Oklahoma oilman who, with a net worth of $11 billion, was ranked number 30 on the *Forbes* list of the richest Americans in 2012. He summed it up well: "We live in an amazing country—because of our capitalist society and free enterprise system, I was able to work my way out of poverty. This process really began in high school when I discovered my passion for the oil and gas industry. My success in the industry has given me opportunities to help others discover and pursue their passions in life." And how does one help others do that? In Hamm's words we glimpse the essential aspects of opportunity: "My family's philanthropic pledge will benefit the life passions for which my wife, Sue Ann, and I care so much: improving health care and educational opportunities for people in the U.S. and throughout the world. We are primarily focused on people whose poverty limits their health care and educational opportunities."[13]

Some signatories even acknowledge the extent to which luck propelled them from being simply rich to being superrich. George B. Kaiser of Tulsa, Oklahoma, wrote, "My good fortune was not due to superior personal character or initiative so much as it was to dumb luck. I was blessed to be born in an advanced society with caring parents. So I had the advantage of both genetics (winning the 'ovarian lottery') and upbringing." Kaiser goes on to identify something much more important: "America's 'social contract' is equal opportunity."[14] Indeed, the notion of equal opportunity may be the most important of all bourgeois values in America because it allows the country to use the economic opportunities available there and not available in other societies to justify, and thus sustain, inequalities inherent in a free market.

How will the Giving Pledge change the future in both the United States and the world? The amount of money still not committed is huge. Hundreds of the wealthy have not signed the pledge or set up foundations to help change the world. For example, Steve Jobs, Apple's founder, who passed away on October 5, 2011, was one of the most beloved people on the planet. He was a visionary, an inventor, a genius. He was also one of the richest men in the world. But he declined to sign the Giving Pledge, and had no public record of any philanthropic activities.[15]

## The Seeds of American Generosity

The modern articulation of philanthropy began with Andrew Carnegie's essay "Wealth," but the roots of American philanthropy go back much further and are planted in the cultural and religious traditions of Americans, who were both self-reliant and bound to community. They embraced capitalism in the New World and rejected the aristocratic and class-bound structure of the Old World. As Alexis de Tocqueville wrote, "In no other country in the world is the love of property keener or more alert than in the United States, and nowhere else does the majority display less inclination toward doctrines which in any way threaten the way property is owned."[16] How are these shared attachments reconciled? The same paradox is reflected in the marriage of tooth-and-nail capitalism with exceptional levels of philanthropy by wealthy Americans. It may seem paradoxical that America can be devoted to both private property and communal activity.

The historian David Fischer, in his cultural history of the United States, argues that British "folkways"—the inherited values and cultures of a society—established enduring attitudes toward wealth and social class. Consider first the exodus of Puritans from eastern England to Massachusetts and of Quakers from the North Midlands of England and Wales to the Delaware Valley in the seventeenth and eighteenth centuries. Attitudes toward wealth among these settlers were not ingrained by the old class divisions of British society, but instead were shaped by more egalitarian conceptions of wealth and inheritance. Fischer argues that these characteristics, or "folkways," which were brought over by early settlers such as the Puritans and Quakers as early as the seventeenth century and which had been fortified by the early nineteenth century, became "the most powerful determinant of a voluntary society in the United States today."[17]

These Puritan principles also influenced the way that land and resources were divided. Throughout Massachusetts in the seventeenth century, landholdings were divided up so that there was not huge diversity. There were also very few land tenants, and in some towns none at all. In Wallingford, Connecticut, for example, land was divided such that "every 'high rank man' received 400 acres; every 'middle rank man' received 300 acres and every 'low rank man' received 200 acres."[18] It's worth noting that many of the low-rank men had been quite destitute in England. Of course, land distribution varied from town to town in New England, although the more "radical" the religious principles of a town, the more it tended toward greater equality of distribution. In general, the "large landless proletariat" of England had no equivalent in the towns and countryside of New England.

In terms of inheritance, in cases where there wasn't a will, laws tended to require that estates be split equally among children, as opposed to all wealth going to the eldest son, as had largely been the English tradition. The men would tend to get the land and women would get the moveable possessions of the family, such as furniture and silverware. In studies of wills, these practices were actually implemented surprisingly often: families with more than one child would split the inheritance equally among their children. Another study of Massachusetts towns from 1630 to 1750 found that the wealthiest 10 percent of people owned only 20 to 30 percent of taxable land. The degree to which the British aristocratic class system had been leveled in the New England colonies was dramatic. One wealthy foreigner visiting from the Old World in 1765 put it best when he observed in a rather disapproving way, "the leveling principle here, everywhere, operates strongly and takes the lead. Everybody has property and everybody knows it."[19]

The Quaker colonies in the Delaware Valley developed with a similar aversion to the old class system. William Penn set out to distribute property so as to avoid creating vast inequalities in wealth. The Quakers created egalitarian landholdings in Pennsylvania, where there were very low levels of inequality from the earliest arrivers to well into the eighteenth century. The Quaker tradition of inheritance was equal division of the estate among the children.

Giving to the needy was also part of the fabric of colonial America. It primarily took the form of direct help to those in need, or of giving money to charitable institutions that took on that responsibility. The act of giving at that time fell primarily within the paradigm of charity, but some did use their fortunes to help build social infrastructure and institutions to address the ills of society. But in addition to charity, philanthropic activity in institution building was clearly evident in eighteenth-century New England. To build social capital—in other words, religion, education, science, cultural etiquette, and the rule of law—the pillars of the community needed to be supported. Opportunity for the middle class was a new idea, and the institutions that would support this were not yet in place.

In 1742, Peter Faneuil funded the building of Boston's public marketplace and meeting hall, Faneuil Hall, which later became known as the "Cradle of Liberty" because of the role it played as a meeting place for those planning revolutionary activities leading up to the Revolutionary War. Peter Faneuil was born in 1700 and had been a prosperous trader of fish, produce, and rum. He was a careful bookkeeper and used innovative methods of risk sharing with other investors. By the age of forty, he was one of the wealthiest men in the colonies and lived prominently in one of Boston's Beacon Hill mansions. Faneuil died young from dropsy in 1743, but his generosity had gained a reputation and in his eulogy it was noted that he "fed the hungry and he clothed the naked, he comforted the fatherless, and the widows in their affliction." An obituary noted that he was "a gentleman, possessed of a very ample fortune and a most generous spirit," and praised his "noble benefaction to his town and constant employment of a great number of tradesmen, artificers, and laborers, to whom he was a liberal paymaster."[20]

Not long after Faneuil's death, the founding fathers decided to frame the country around a national creed rather than a national history, thus further binding its future to an inclusive American identity. America's founding fathers defined its raison d'être: "It has been our fate as a nation not to have ideologies, but to be one." According to the political sociologist Seymour Martin Lipset, a longtime student of American exceptionalism, the "American Creed" can be described in five terms: liberty, egalitarianism, individualism, populism, and laissez-faire government. The very idea of a national creed that comes from a shared ideology, as opposed to an exclusive ethnic division or national history, was unique. National histories, of course, have been powerful rallying cries for divisive and nationalistic politics. In the new American nation, class structure and hierarchy were less important than they were in the rule-bound aristocratic societies left behind in the Old World.

## Southern Folkways: Slavery and the Aristocracy

Although it is tempting to conclude from the discussion in the previous section that the entire American experiment was a rejection of the hereditary class system of Britain, the South is a major exception to this general trend. Slavery in America, of course, is antithetical to much of the history I have discussed so far, as is the system of large plantation farms that dominated the organization of land in the South. Indeed, both aspects of Southern society are fundamentally at odds with any narrative about opportunity.

The system of slavery can be traced back to a different current, distinct from the largely Puritan and Quaker settlements of the North. As Fischer argues, it can be traced back to one man, Sir William Berkeley, and his recruiting campaign to bring Royalists from England to colonize Virginia in the image of the English country estate. Berkeley was born to a prominent and influential family that had been in power since the eleventh century in the imposing Berkeley Castle, which still stands in Gloucestershire, England. He had been educated at Queen's College, Oxford, and, having a flair for poetry, he stayed on to become a fellow at Merton College and in 1639 even published a "tragic comedy" titled *The Lost Lady*.[21]

At the end of the English Civil War, around 1650, Royalists from southern England began to join the migration to the New World, bringing with them aristocratic attitudes toward wealth and property that embraced inequality. So, unlike the Puritan and Quaker establishments in the northern colonies, the South, from its most formative years under the rule of Sir Berkeley up until the American Civil War, was dominated by large estates and a ruling oligarchy—the antithesis of an entrepreneurial society.

Many of the Royalist settlers, or "cavaliers," were the second sons of prominent families in southwest England who founded what would later be called the first families of Virginia. Historians have referred to Virginia's "younger son syndrome" to describe the migratory patterns of these wealthy but displaced men who had to look elsewhere for opportunity; they were wealthy, but they could not inherit their families' vast estates. Many had been educated in classics at the Royalist colleges Merton and Christ Church at Oxford.

From 1642 to 1675, a small Royalist elite immigrated from southern England to Virginia, bringing large numbers of indentured servants and criminals to work on their large plantations, where they produced cash crops. These solid Episcopalians and Anglicans, who forbade an education to their servants, also brought slavery to the American South.[22]

By 1850, on the eve of the Civil War, the United States was more or less divided into three economic systems: the increasingly urban and industrialized North, the plantation economy of the South, and the relatively egalitarian social structure of the Midwestern farmlands. These three modes of economic and social organization had evolved from these regions' social and cultural histories. As the historian Barrington Moore starkly put it when describing the South just prior to the Civil War, "Southern society was based firmly on hereditary status as the basis of human worth."[23] In many ways, the South had evolved in a way that was incompatible with a system that was an "heir of the Puritan, American, and French Revolutions." Indeed, this became abundantly clear in the many calls for breaking down the entire social structure of the South following its defeat. This was not, however, to satisfy abolitionist or progressive goals, but rather because the system of large hereditary plantations of the South was incompatible with the goals of Northern industrial capitalism.

When the South lost the war, some Republican politicians denounced it as an anachronistic remnant of a dying world of "baron and serf—noble and slave."[24] There were even calls by more radical Northern Republicans to completely reorder Southern society by dividing up the plantations and redistributing the land. The Republican politician Thaddeus Stevens, speaking on behalf of a coalition of industrialists and labor, wanted to break up every Southern estate larger than two hundred acres.

These calls emanated from an alliance of reformists and industrialists, not because this faction of Republicans was particularly egalitarian, but rather because the system of plantations was antithetical to the interests of Northern industrialists, who saw huge economic opportunities if the South were to adopt a capitalist system. Breaking down the plantation system and displacing the interests of plantation owners in local economics and national politics could have bestowed huge advantages on Northern industrialists.

The old system of economic organization persisted in the South, however, and slaves became sharecroppers—thus, in an economic sense, mimicking the old feudal system that capitalism had done so much to dismantle elsewhere in the Western world.

## Voluntary Society

As Tocqueville observed in the early nineteenth century, "The Americans enjoy explaining almost every act of their lives on the principle of self-interest properly understood. It gives them great pleasure to point out how an enlightened self-love continually leads them to help one another and disposes them freely to give part of their time and wealth for the good of the state."[25] Volunteerism, associations, and self-reliance are also related to this sense of community and shared interests.

Early evidence of giving habits among working-class Americans suggests that donating money was ingrained in the habits of vast numbers of Americans. In 1908, the Department of Labor conducted a survey of workers with average incomes. The survey found that, on average, 1.5 percent of a worker's income was given to the church and other charitable causes, and 1.8 percent was given to other voluntary associations. Another 0.4 percent was given away in more informal ways to friends and family. These figures closely match similar budgets of the working class compiled by the U.S. Bureau of Labor Statistics.[26] During the early twentieth century, many of the causes supported by the working class were probably local, and it's unclear whether these causes tended to be more charitable or philanthropic in nature. Regardless, tendencies toward giving and volunteering were firmly established among Americans of varying classes.

Both philanthropy and volunteerism are about twice as common in the United States as they are, on average, in other countries.[27] Today, philanthropy and volunteering are related forms of altruism. According to Robert Putnam, volunteering is one of the strongest predictors of philanthropy and vice versa. College-educated Americans are more than twice as likely to volunteer as those with only high school diplomas. It is not a matter of income, however: the poor give, as a fraction of their income, at about the same rate as middle-class Americans and at a somewhat lower rate than

the wealthy.[28] Many religious faiths in the United States encourage volunteering. Today, the U.S. religious tradition is
especially strong, particularly when compared to Western
European countries with similar levels of development.

## Mass Philanthropy

The community organizations that Tocqueville described
were reflected in the mass giving that burgeoned during
the twentieth century. During that time, mass philanthropy
became more institutionalized, with large-scale campaigns
that used volunteers to canvass every town and city in the
country. In some ways, this marked a shift from the dominance of local charities to more nationalized efforts. I remember the March of Dimes movement when I was growing up. The March of Dimes collected money in small clear
containers with a metal top and a slot to insert a dime. Each
container would hold one hundred dimes, or ten dollars.
We would walk around the neighborhood collecting dimes
from all of our neighbors. March of Dimes was different
from early examples of philanthropy and charity because it
was national in scope and high organized. Also, the cause
was less to aid those who had been crippled by polio than
to support scientific research that would develop a cure.
Indeed, reformers, such as public health advocates and social workers, have looked to the largesse of the wealthiest
Americans as well as to the gifts of everyday workers as
they broadened the appeal of mass philanthropy.

Mass philanthropy has also been prominent in higher
education. In large part, this started when research universities linked themselves into larger cultural movements to
repackage their staid image. This shift in the mass appeal

and public prominence of universities no doubt contributed to the growing number of small philanthropic contributions that together account for the staggeringly large endowments of many American universities.

For example, William Rainey Harper, whom I introduced earlier as the man Rockefeller appointed to run the newly founded University of Chicago, wanted the university to represent the city of Chicago, which was quickly becoming the social and economic hub of the Midwest as it transitioned from frontier life to a densely populated, industrial urban center.[29] Harper implemented a strategy to make the University of Chicago a rallying point. He used the 1893 World's Fair as an opportunity to erect stunning campus buildings in the Beaux Arts style. Rockefeller's Standard Oil Company built an oil rig on campus, and offered postcards to World Fair visitors so they would share the greatness of University of Chicago, the city, and Standard Oil with family and friends all over the world. The fair celebrated the four hundredth anniversary of Columbus's arrival in North America and, more important, the transformation of the United States into an industrial power. Harper did his utmost to ensure that the University of Chicago would come to represent that emerging strength.

Harper also enticed Alonzo Stagg, who had been an all-American football player at Yale and was developing a prominent reputation as a coach, to leave Yale and lead the University of Chicago football team. College football was wildly popular even then, and the team's success under Stagg created insatiable public demand for news stories. The success of the football team tied the city and the region to the university.[30]

Harper made the University of Chicago a central institution in the dynamic, expanding metropolitan area. In many ways he created the prototype for the modern American research university that was heavily integrated into the surrounding community's social and economic fabric. Harper's model of providing scientific and commercial influence while also promoting the public good through educational offerings, sports, exhibitions, and civic engagement would prove to be a hallmark of the great American research universities.

## The Welfare State and the Persistence of Philanthropy

One striking feature of American philanthropy is its persistence throughout the twentieth century, even as the state grew to extraordinary size. The period of entrepreneurship and philanthropy in the nineteenth century was followed by a period of Progressivism in the early twentieth century and during World War I, which meant an increased role of government in social welfare.

The government took on a larger role in education, health, and retirement support. Although the 1920s was a decade of technological change and prosperity, underlying economic problems resulted in the collapse of the world economy and the Great Depression in the 1930s. The interwar period and World War II, with their high taxes and antitrust laws, changed the role of government and entrepreneurs' philanthropic activities.

It is interesting that the rise of the welfare state in the United States did not coincide with a decline in philanthropy. In fact, total private domestic philanthropy as a percentage of GDP increased between 1929 and 1959, from

1.7 percent to 2.3 percent. It averaged 2.1 percent during this period.[31] This figure is not significantly different from the 2.5 percent of GDP that Americans contributed to philanthropic causes in 1997.

So why did Americans continue to fund philanthropy at a constant level, even as the federal government stepped into the business of social security? According to *Newsweek,*

> There's no escaping the brutal truth: the nation famous for capitalism red in tooth and claw, the epicenter of the heartless marketplace, is also the land of the handout. It's not really such a paradox. Both our entrepreneurial economic system and our philanthropic tradition spring from the same root: American individualism. Other countries may be content to let the government run most of their schools and universities, pay for their hospitals, subsidize their museums and orchestras, even in some cases support religious sects. Americans tend to think most of these institutions are best kept in private hands, and they have been willing to cough up the money to pay for them.[32]

The answer to our question seems to be American exceptionalism. America is different from any other nation.

## Political Philanthropy

Charitable and philanthropic contributions cover a wide range of causes. The focus of this book has been on contributions that create opportunity. So far, I have focused on the creation and support of private research universities in the United States, K–12 education, and research initiatives.

It would be naïve, however, to think that all philanthropic contributions are equally suited to contribute to opportunity. Philanthropy cannot be controlled, so the causes to which money flows depend on the currents and cultures of those with wealth.

Since it first appeared, philanthropy has been enmeshed in political and ideological struggles. There are some eighteen hundred think tanks today, many of which are funded by philanthropists who wish to influence debate over public policies. Going back to the Cold War, for example, the Ford Foundation and other American foundations were actively involved in trying to win the ideological war with the Soviet Union. Sometimes these foundations worked in partnership with the U.S. government and sometimes they acted alone, pursuing an anti-Communist ideology.

In recent years, other philanthropists have used their money to support political campaigns and advocacy in the United States. The Koch brothers, who have not signed the Giving Pledge, made their fortune in manufacturing and energy. Are they engaged in creating opportunity in America? Many would argue that the Koch brothers are actively involved in just the opposite: using their wealth to deprive Americans of opportunity by supporting antiunion activities, limited government, and right-wing activities conducted by the Mercatus Center at George Mason University and other institutions. Although David Koch has donated six hundred million dollars to the arts and medical research since 2000, this is a small amount of money relative to the family fortune.

For more than three centuries, American philanthropy has been trying to create a better society. This goal is consistent with the wishes of the founding fathers and has been central to the nation's commitment to that vision. Great fortunes have been used to that end with great success in America. Great fortunes should not be used to promote personal or class interests.

## Why Philanthropy?

Generations of economists have cited Adam Smith, the founder of modern economics, when proclaiming the prominent role self-interest plays in motivating human activity. Nonetheless, even Smith recognized that society does not progress through self-interest alone. Economists have largely ignored Smith's *Theory of Moral Sentiments*, which predates *The Wealth of Nations* by nearly two decades and which few students read today. Smith opens the former with this passage: "How selfish soever man may be supposed, there are evidently some principles of his nature, which interest him in the fortune of others, and render their happiness necessary to him, though he derives nothing from it, except the pleasure of seeing it."[33]

Economists try to explain altruism as enlightened self-interest, quoting Smith's *Wealth of Nations*: "It is not from the benevolence of the butcher, the brewer, or the baker, that we expect our dinner, but from their regard to their own interest."[34]

On one level, economists could claim that the behavior Smith describes is consistent with modern-day economics. After all, modern economics postulates that each individual derives happiness from the available choices of how to spend one's income. The "rational" consumer will allocate his or her money so that the benefit from each dollar is the same. As the great economist Kenneth Boulding expressed it, "That liberty cannot be established without morality, nor morality without faith," is a fundamental fact of American exception-alism.[35] Economists from the time of Adam Smith have rec-ognized the power of self-interest in the creation of wealth.

The Nobel Prize winner Herbert A. Simon echoes Bould-ing's view, stating that "economics assumes that people maximize happiness but postulates nothing about what hap-piness is. With only this assumption, it is impossible to dis-tinguish altruism from selfishness."[36] Simon proposes a defi-nition of altruism as a "sacrifice of fitness," meaning that we give something up for the survival of others. It then becomes possible to determine which choices are selfish and which are altruistic by examining the impact of a million-dollar gift. Whom did it benefit? How many people? Economic the-ory has treated economic gain as the primary human motive for every action, but an empirically grounded theory would assign comparable weight to other motives, including altru-ism and the organizational identification associated with it.[37]

When economists confront philanthropic behavior, they generally look for the quid pro quo behind the act—in other words, what's in it for the giver? Hence, economists conclude that behavior that appears altruistic is fundamen-tally consistent with self-interest. Contemporary economic theory, with notable exceptions, has largely ignored the pos-sibility of altruistic behavior. A contrasting view is offered by the sociologists who conducted a survey of the theory and research on altruism, which concluded that altruism is a characteristic of human nature.[38]

It is tempting for an economist to argue that there really are no gifts and that all transactions involve some kind of exchange, that is, some kind of quid pro quo. If we drop a dime in the blind man's cup, it is because the blind man gives us something. We feel a certain glow of emotional vir-tue, and it is this that we receive for our dime.

Is philanthropic behavior, then, always motivated by self-interest? Is there always a quid pro quo? If the former is true, then the self-interested motive argued by economists is justified. If there is no quid pro quo, the question arises whether the returns to society are greater when philanthropic behavior requires none.

The idea that philanthropy is no different from self-interested behavior is seriously misleading, however, because nothing requires all motivations to be alike. Indeed, the motivation that leads to philanthropic behavior "may be very different from that which leads us to build up a personal estate or to purchase consumer goods for our own use."[39] If we regard an individual's philanthropic donations as an expression of a "sense of community with others," then behavior that seems irrational or mysterious to economists becomes less so.[40]

The vitality of American-style capitalism is a testament to the importance of behavior that is not motivated by self-interest. Hence, an economic theory that ignores altruistic behavior does not reflect the real world. I suggest that altruism is superior to enlightened self-interest and believe that American exceptionalism provides an example of this, which is crucial to our nation's prosperity because without the common good in mind, we do only what is good for ourselves.

In most cases, we will probably never know why philanthropists give. Certainly, some prominent philanthropists, like Andrew Carnegie, have written forcefully explaining why they give, thus providing some insights. Even when the words are written down, however, as observers of philanthropic giving we can never truly know what drives these individuals.

Consider that, from the perspective of the philanthropist, philanthropy could be either consumption spending or investment. On the consumption side, we know, for example, that people can spend a lot of money to dress in a certain way in order to be perceived as wealthy, stylish, or the like. Similarly, those with a lot of money may treat getting their names on buildings or in the newspaper as a consumption item. It would be foolish to suggest that those whose names have been emblazoned on research facilities on many campuses in recent years don't get particular satisfaction from having their generosity recognized. At Princeton, there is the Carl C. Icahn Genomics Laboratory. At Duke, there is the Levine Science Research Center, named after Leon Levine, the founder and CEO of the Family Dollar discount store chain. At Johns Hopkins, Michael Bloomberg donated money to what became the Bloomberg School of Public Health. The list goes on and on.

The issue is interesting because some philanthropists go out of their way to remain anonymous. In fact, many of the rich try to fly under the radar for a number of reasons. If one gives anonymously, that seems to undermine both the exchange argument and the consumption argument.

It seems perfectly reasonable that philanthropy could be viewed as consumption for the megawealthy, and not exclusively tied to altruistic behavior. The wealthy want to be recognized for their contributions because they live in a society that reveres generosity. If their peers thought it foolish to use their fortunes for philanthropic purposes, it would seem that philanthropy would be a much less popular consumption item.

## Conclusion

The history of philanthropy in the United States discussed in this chapter suggests that some of the philanthropic impulses that developed in America in the eighteenth and

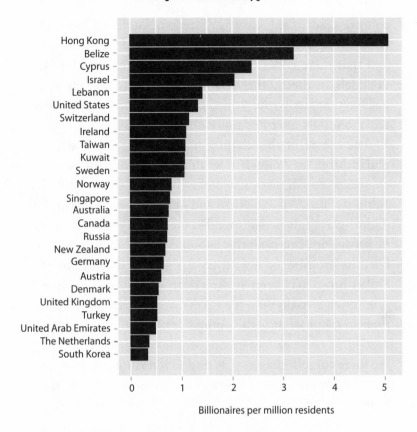

**Figure 3**. Billionaires per Million Residents by Country
*Source:* Compiled by author.

nineteenth centuries can be traced back to the religious
and cultural values of English immigrant communities. England is actually the second most generous country after the
United States, when considering giving as a percentage of
GDP. The United States is not the only country with a large
number of billionaires, however. On a per capita basis, the
United States in recent years has ranked about sixth in the
number of billionaires per capita, behind Hong Kong, Be-
lize, Cyprus, Israel, and Lebanon (see figure 3). And other

countries such as Norway, Sweden, Germany, and the United Kingdom fall right behind the United States. So why is it that there is not more philanthropy from wealthy individuals in these other countries? There is no reason to believe that the wealthy in the United States should have any monopoly over institutionalized giving.

The theme of this chapter has been the abundance of philanthropy in America over time and compared to other countries. I've argued that philanthropy is woven into the cultural fabric of America and into the entrepreneurial middle-class values that founded the country and sustained its prosperity. But is all this enough? Has philanthropy fulfilled its promise, or does it have a greater distance to go? Philanthropy has been an American response to the question of what to do with the excess wealth created by entrepreneurs. But what is the optimal amount of philanthropy needed in order to create opportunity without disrupting the forces of self-interest that lead to innovation and wealth in the first place? These questions are the focus of the next chapter.

# CHAPTER 6

# AMERICAN-STYLE CAPITALISM

*The world is not so governed from above that private and social
interest always coincide. It is not so managed here below that in
practice they coincide.*

—JOHN MAYNARD KEYNES

## Philanthropy and Capitalism

In chapter 1 I closed with a question, "Is American-style
capitalism working?" Of course to answer that question we
need to be clear about what exactly American-style capitalism is. And the answer to that depends on who one asks.
In chapters 2–5 I tried to paint a broad-brush picture of
what I think are the currents of American capitalism: opportunity, entrepreneurship, wealth creation, and philanthropy. Using this metaphor of the currents, let's now use a
finer brush and paint a more nuanced picture of American
prosperity today.

How could philanthropy be a part of capitalism? Capitalism is a relatively orderly system, governed by the trac-
table logic of supply and demand. Philanthropy, by contrast, lacks a set of laws to explain its ebbs and flows. Like
the charities and arts patronages in royal courts throughout

European history, philanthropy is subject to the whims of the wealthy. Furthermore, philanthropy is not only largely ungoverned by economic principles but also relatively free from the checks and balances of democracy, such as elections, referendums, and recalls.

As discussed in chapter 5, it is not easy for social scientists to understand exactly why philanthropy exists—except as a tax shelter (which would make it a rational response to tax policy) or as consumption (the price to get one's name on a building). As I've tried to demonstrate, however, American philanthropy defies such easy explanations. Philanthropy as a way to avoid taxes does not explain why the richest three Americans have agreed to give away at least 95 percent of their wealth. Philanthropy as a consumption good does not explain the millions of cases of anonymous contributions that underpin America's long history of mass philanthropy.

Philanthropy has long been a powerful force for social change, often viewed as moving on a parallel track with capitalism. Rarely is it understood as an entity intertwined with American capitalism. Yet, it has both emanated from the capitalist system and continually nurtured the system. It is a product of capitalism—another way in which industrialists have sought to shape American society and values. Thus, Ewing Marion Kauffman not only influenced American life with the mass production of pharmaceuticals but also imposed his worldview on society through the millions spent by the Kauffman Foundation of Kansas City to promote entrepreneurship and education. Such is the audacity of American capitalism.

Historically, philanthropy has been loyal to the institutions of American capitalism. This has been most evident in the institutions supporting opportunity creation and innovation: philanthropists have invested fortunes in schools, universities, libraries, and research centers. The strength of American capitalism depends on the health of these institutions and on their ability to produce new ideas and train new workers for the marketplace. Thus, philanthropy and capitalism are symbiotic, with the strength of one reinforcing the strength of the other and vice versa.

American philanthropists presumably value a strong capitalist system because it is the system that nurtured their individual success. Thus, they seem to recognize that the strength of American capitalism resides neither in the size or influence of an industry or a set of firms nor in a country's GDP. Rather, as philanthropists have put it, the strength of capitalism is measured in a more aspirational way. Opportunity allows individuals to participate in the economic system and keeps the door open for new ideas and new firms. Innovation follows from opportunity: it is what you get when you take smart, educated people and allow them to solve problems.

In America, the absence of opportunity takes two forms. First, it's manifested in places like failing secondary schools, where students fall behind the norm early and never catch up, thus being shut out of successful participation in the economy. Second, it's also apparent in failures of innovation like the Hush-A-Phone debacle described in chapter 3. When a Harvard-educated sound engineer and an ambitious entrepreneur are put out of business because a company like Bell is nervous about competition or an agency like the FCC holds fast to an arcane rule, the institutions supporting opportunity are clearly inadequate. Philanthropy does not solve all of these problems, but the way in which philanthropy recycles wealth—and invests it in new generations and new ideas—reflects a system that values a dynamic form of opportunity as opposed to something fixed or exclusionary.

If you look at foundations, which make up only a fraction of American philanthropy, a quarter of the money goes to education and another quarter goes to medicine, science, and other research goals. In an alternative universe, philanthropists could spend all of their money on oil paintings and medieval armor collections and use foundations as little more than vehicles to loan their priceless belongings to galleries for the public's edification. Some wealthy Americans do this, but most don't. American philanthropy has been remarkably focused on strengthening the institutions undergirding the success of American capitalism.

Philanthropy has also addressed the issue of wealth in America. When capitalism is really innovative, it generates huge amounts of wealth, often for a relatively small number of people. There is no problem with this, other things being equal, unless the wealth stays idle. As Keynes comments, "The love of money as a possession . . . . will be recognized for what it is, a somewhat disgusting morbidity."[1] As the English nobility demonstrated, idle wealth does little to advance capitalism. When wealth is not recycled to strengthen the systems of opportunity and innovation, the long-term health of capitalism suffers. Countries with the so-called resource curse have this problem today. Oil and mineral elites have no incentive to reinvest their money to create systems of opportunity and innovation in their own society. Part of the problem is that such elites did not come by their money through innovation and opportunity, as I've defined these terms, but rather through violence, bribery, and other forms of malfeasance. The wealthy tend to show allegiance to the system that sustains them, whether it's entrepreneurship, inheritance, or corruption.

The American institutions of opportunity and innovation are well developed today, but they owe their origination to local and independent efforts. Early Americans in New England and the Chesapeake region, and later throughout the West, established schools in the vast majority of towns and villages. There was no legal requirement to do this, nor any norm adapted from other countries. Among white Americans, the literacy rate was arguably the highest in the world by 1800. It is probably a stretch to argue that all of these schools were created by capitalists. Rather, it's likely that these schools were created mostly by a mix of farmers, local businessmen, and religious leaders who wanted to strengthen the standing of their towns or villages. Such institution building is reflected in philanthropy—a system that is as aspirational as it is independent.

In Western Europe, where there is far less philanthropy, the capitalist system is supported almost entirely by the state. The reason this alternative equilibrium occurred in Europe seems likely to be derived from some mix of culture and history. Although countries such as France do have foundations and nonprofits, such as the famed Médecins sans Frontières, these efforts largely support institution building *outside* of the country. It is difficult to find examples where European philanthropy has actually strengthened institutions of capitalism in Europe. Rather, European philanthropy, for complex reasons, has always avoided competing with the state in the provision of services and the support of native institutions. Thus, philanthropy goes in search of alternative locales, often where there is more room to breathe.

In America, philanthropy and government have been more willing to compete on their home turf. The government has shown devotion to the institutions of capitalism—those that sustain opportunity creation and innovation. Many of these examples have been highlighted already: the system of public schooling, developed piecemeal by the states and later by the federal government; the land-grant universities; and the National Science Foundation and the National Institutes of Health. Philanthropy and volunteerism have been largely in sync with these state efforts, sometimes collaborating and sometimes competing, but almost always strengthening the overarching goals of fostering opportunity and innovation.

## Changes in American Capitalism

In this book, I have described American capitalism as a system that relies on opportunity, innovation, wealth, and philanthropy. Others have described capitalism in very different terms, often by highlighting the role of particular institutions, such as industries, unions, and government, or by making pronouncements that the size of government, all else being equal, determines whether or not capitalism can exist.[2] Yet, as I have tried to demonstrate in this book, what defines American capitalism has little to do with whether the government spends, for example, 30 percent or 40 percent of GDP—the difference between the United States and Germany in recent years. Instead, American capitalism has much more to do with the strength of these core institutions.

Over its history, however, American capitalism has gone through different phases. One might argue that it has *evolved*, although this would imply that it keeps getting better. The challenge in assessing the trajectory of American capitalism is that features of the global economy are constantly changing, and thus an ideal system in one decade may be disastrous in another. In chapter 3, I highlighted the changes in American capitalism throughout its history, but most dramatically during the period from the late nineteenth century, when the industrial revolution was under way, to the late twentieth century, when many features of the managed economy unraveled. My central argument is that American capitalism has moved from one Gilded Age to another, with a period in between that I call the managed economy, which contained many attractive but unsustainable features. The managed economy was different not because government was big, but because of how government and business conducted their affairs *together*.

During the health-care debate across the United States early in Obama's presidency many observers declared that American capitalism was going through another evolution—socialism. Similar charges were made against Roosevelt's government during the New Deal era. As long as health-care providers, pharmaceutical companies, and hospitals still have an incentive to innovate, however, nothing fundamental about American capitalism will actually change. Most serious observers understand this. Even though the health-care law promises to increase the share of government spending as a percentage of GDP, the highly competitive and innovative system of American capitalism would be largely untouched.

The managed economy of the postwar era—known intimately by baby boomers like me—was the most antithetical to the American model. One reason for this is that America was experiencing an unrealistically long period of strong economic growth. The rest of the world had been devastated by war and American industry was strong and expanding after a period of intensive innovation and entrepreneurship. The United States was able to ride this wave, so to speak, from the immediate postwar period until about the 1970s, when the system unraveled. Around this time, business leaders, politicians, entrepreneurs, and other elites recognized that the relationship between big business and government was not going to be sustainable, particularly if competition from Japan, Germany, and other rapidly rising economic powers persisted.

The United States dismantled the managerial economy piece by piece—in ways planned and unplanned—largely by severing the relationships between government agencies and businesses and allowing new and innovative firms to challenge the hegemony of the old. To some degree, this strengthened the institutions of opportunity, innovation, wealth, and philanthropy, but in other ways it confronted them with new challenges.

As the managerial economy tumbled, smaller firms could look around and recognize that they had considerably more opportunity than previously. They were able to raise money, particularly in the high-tech fields, and they were able to take advantage of much of the research coming out of universities, thanks to a series of new laws. This resurgence of opportunity for new ideas and new collaborative efforts between entrepreneurs, financiers, and a new high-tech culture ran in tandem with growth in economic opportunity. With opportunity and innovation came wealth. The stock market has grown dramatically since the early 1980s, creating vast amounts of wealth for the owners of capital. In theory, the American economy of late has been wide open, with plenty of money to be made by those with drive and the capacity to innovate. From a different vantage point, however, changes in the economy have unfolded like a twisted game of musical chairs, in which some players are invited into the room after the music has already stopped.


## The New Gilded Age (America since the 1970s)

In many respects, America seems to have quietly settled into a new Gilded Age over the past thirty years. This has happened across Democratic and Republican administrations and, until the Great Recession, largely without the fanfare of new political parties, mass protests, or sustained unrest within the system. Like the first Gilded Age at the end of the nineteenth century, many of the wealthier participants in the economy have fared extremely well. The frontiers of high technology, finance, and medicine continue to be productive and innovative. Nonetheless, behind the veneer of success it's clear that the institutions of opportunity and innovation are not working well enough for everyone. Median incomes have been flat since the 1970s and the difference in wealth between the poorest and richest Americans has steadily been increasing over this period.

In recent years, the economic crisis has hit middle-class Americans very hard. Between the fall of 2008 and the summer of 2009, four and a half million jobs were lost and the unemployment rate doubled to 10 percent. America lost seven hundred thousand jobs a month for six months in a row. Moreover, jobs did not return and the number of long-term unemployed continued to climb. This is usually the situation when a financial crisis is followed by an economic recession.[3] Total employment in 2012 is still below the 2008 figure.

Although many jobs have been shed during the Great Recession, American businesses have evolved to become more productive, no doubt partly in response to the increased competition brought on by globalization. If you look at the rate of productivity growth, which over the long run determines improvements in average living standards, the recent years have been fairly amazing. Between 1995 and 2002, the rate of productivity growth in the United States was 2.8 percent per year—the highest sustained rate ever recorded. By 2005, it had reached an even higher rate of a little more than 3 percent per year.

Why is this important? Living standards double every twenty-eight years at a rate of 2.6 percent annual growth in productivity, whereas this doubling would take more than fifty years at a rate of 1.4 percent. What accounts for America's good fortune so far? Conventional economic wisdom has converged around the opinion that the information revolution—especially the rapidly falling price of computer chips and related products—has been critical. When measured by conventional statistics, there seems to be a great deal of truth to this. Between 1993 and 2003, productivity in the electronics products manufacturing sector grew at an average annual rate of 15 percent, compared to an average of 4 percent for manufacturing as a whole. The decades-long structural transition from a managed economy to an entrepreneurial society seems to have played an important role in the acceleration of economic growth.[4]

The cowboy capitalism of the past thirty years has brought extraordinary changes to the economy. The corporate raiders of the 1980s and the Mitt Romneys at Bain Capital and other private equity firms are an extreme example, but they represent willingness for the economy to be recreated. Less salient are the multitudes of small manufacturing firms, innovations in retail, developers of software applications, and recent advances in telecommunications that have challenged the hegemony of established firms. These radical changes in the economy are the product of *economic* opportunity. They give upstarts a chance and help to make the economy more nimble and efficient, which should help the United States compete globally.[5]

Part of the problem is that much of the new wealth does not create jobs and thus by itself does not create opportunity for average Americans. Consider the financial industry, where there have been lots of innovations but few of these innovations have made life better for average Americans, though they have helped make markets more efficient globally. Even the companies that do touch Americans have created few jobs. Consider that, as I write this, Facebook has a market capitalization of about sixty-five billion dollars and employs about 3,500 people. When companies during the industrial revolution had market capitalizations comparable to Facebook's, they created tens of thousands of jobs. Thus, although entrepreneurship is still good for wealth creation, today we need ten Mark Zuckerbergs for each John Rockefeller if we are interested in job creation.

In addition to creating opportunities for new firms, the new Gilded Age economy has proved very good at increasing the number of consumer choices one has: a new iPhone model comes out approximately every year. Yet, this does not imply an increase in opportunity for Americans. This is perhaps a paradox of capitalism over the past few decades in America. Entrepreneurs have grown increasingly good at producing new and dazzling goods at low cost. Nonetheless, these innovations, while providing some cost savings and new forms of entertainment for consumers, apparently have not created enough meaningful workplace opportunities for those in the job market.

Some might argue that the Gilded Age of the late 1990s was a much better time than the present. After ups and downs in the economy since the mid-1970s, the economy did extraordinarily well through the 1990s. Unemployment was just under 5 percent, the economy was growing at 4 percent a year, inflation was under control, manufacturing productivity was rising, the dollar was strong, and the stock market was breaking records as a matter of course. The United States was riding the early wave of the information revolution, which it had caught first. Yet, as with any good surfing spot, it wouldn't take long for word to get around.[6]

Since the 1990s, the United States has had to endure two poorly managed speculative bubbles: first the dot-com bubble, followed by the prolonged housing fiasco. All the while there has been continued global competition for jobs, particularly in high-end manufacturing and services, with companies in China and India increasingly taking on skilled tasks. In fact, part of what companies like Apple are saying today is that not only do companies in China make high-end electronics more cheaply than American workers, but these companies are more flexible and responsive to needs of firms like Apple, and are able to turn around products quickly. When the late Steve Jobs was asked by President Obama what it would take to bring Apple manufacturing jobs back to the United States, the CEO of Apple replied that those jobs were not coming back.[7]

## Innovation Needed (to Pull Out of Recession)

Philanthropy, like innovation, is aspirational. If society were working optimally, philanthropists would be out of business, so to speak. Similarly, innovation exists to offer something better than the status quo. Perhaps due to these thematic similarities, philanthropists have been particularly devoted to the innovative systems in the United States, funding research institutions, universities, and individuals who show promise.

In the coming decades, it will be interesting to see whether this nexus between innovation and philanthropy grows, particularly as society seems to be placing ever-increasing importance on innovation, and as much of the innovative machinery in the economy has been relocated to universities. As discussed, global competitiveness has significantly undermined the system of corporate research laboratories that reigned supreme for much of the twentieth century. Gone are the days when companies like Xerox, with their near-monopoly status in the marketplace, could afford to support cutting-edge and open-ended research and maintain their dominance in the market. In its heyday the innovative potential of Xerox PARC was undisputed, but that model, as it existed, has been put out of business.

The demise of the corporate industrial laboratories puts increased pressure on American universities to sustain innovation. This is particularly interesting in the context of philanthropy, as universities have been much more the playgrounds of philanthropists than places like Xerox PARC and Bell Labs. Universities are eager to take contributions and they are relatively more willing than big business is to reinvent programs, departments, and partnerships in order to attract new sources of funding and raise their profiles.

Universities allow themselves to be shaped by industrialists and, at the same time, industrialists seem quite interested in shaping the goals and directions of universities. Perhaps it's because universities seem to hold so much promise in the minds of ambitious individuals, without being confined to simple models of success. Thus, philanthropic contributions will likely spur a panoply of initiatives to push universities toward the twenty-first-century changes that mirror the efforts of past centuries yet move in unforeseen directions.

## Universities Needed

Ambitious philanthropists like Leland Stanford and Ezra Cornell could never have foreseen how radically their universities would be reinvented. Nonetheless, they created institutions to serve a particular purpose: to sustain a society that valued learning, innovation, and competition. As I've argued throughout this book, universities like Stanford were built by capitalists to sustain capitalism.

Universities have supported American capitalism in two obvious ways. The first is by helping the workforce keep pace as the economy innovates. In a general sense, industrialists shaped universities to nurture the ambitious—those who can benefit from and strengthen the capitalist system, people just like themselves. The was true for Leland Stanford when he set up his university more than a century ago, and it seems to be true as philanthropy continues to shape the classrooms in Palo Alto today. Philanthropists created a university system that has never really been vocational—although it provides a broad education to scientists and engineers—as much as it has been aspirational, as if to prepare one to take on the world.

The second way universities sustain capitalism is through their contribution to innovation. The U.S. government has long understood this important aspect of higher education and has spent countless sums in grant money strengthening the relationship between universities and innovation, with or without the assistance of philanthropists. The government probably calculates that it got a good return on its investment. Grants to research faculty at places like Stanford both help to educate the next generation of researchers and support the development of new innovations. This is reflected in the budgets of the major American research universities, where about a third of the money these schools spend in a given year goes to the classroom and another quarter goes to supporting the research of faculty and students. Public research universities have a nearly identical breakdown in their budgets. Thus, as this model of funding research universities has evolved over the past five decades, universities have grown increasingly active in competing for grants and attracting star research talent. When the system works, it is a very efficient way to stimulate research.

Yet, despite the government's largesse, without philanthropy American universities would have considerable trouble remaining competitive. On average, the budget of a major *private* research university is supported by four parts, each of roughly equal size: one part philanthropy, one part tuition, one part government grants, and one part miscellaneous income, such as the sale of merchandise, tickets to sports events, and media rights. For *public* universities, the mixture is similarly made of four parts, albeit with about half as much of the budget dependent on philanthropy. Thus, for public universities, roughly 10 percent of revenue comes from philanthropy, compared to roughly 25 percent at private universities. Without question, philanthropic support is crucial to research universities, both public and private, in many cases from their inception to the present.

Much of the funding that comes from large donors is earmarked in some way, tied to a particular initiative such as supporting faculty or facilities in a department, or fostering a new area of research. The many endowed chairs with the names of philanthropists are an example of this, as are buildings like the Carl Icahn Laboratory at Princeton, which houses the Lewis-Sigler Institute for Integrative Genomics.

As Alan Greenspan said, "In the 21st century, our institutions of higher learning will bear the enormous responsibility of ensuring that our society is prepared for the demands of rapid economic change."[8] Indeed, it seems inevitable that American capitalism will continue to shape research universities and small colleges in new ways. Some of these changes will be widely welcomed and others are likely to be controversial, but nonetheless, the model of higher education in the United States has been highly adaptable—in no small part due to the active role played by philanthropy.

Philanthropy's contribution to higher education has grown in recent years. One study found that between 1994 and 2004, philanthropists' contributions to universities increased by 94 percent, or by 84 percent when adjusting for the growth in enrollments. Looking at who was giving, the study found that roughly half of the contributions came from individuals and the other half came from private and corporate foundations. Of the contributions from individuals, roughly half was from alumni and half from non-alumni.[9] It is always difficult to explain such developments in giving. Perhaps the success of the stock market played a role in expanding philanthropic giving, or perhaps the growth in the number of rich entrepreneurs of late explains the increase in higher education philanthropy. This latter possibility would be consistent with many of the philanthropic initiatives during the first Gilded Age.

Philanthropic contributions also have the potential to transform the relationship between universities and the private sector. One radical idea is to allow companies to further leverage the research capacity of universities. Such arrangements usually involve the university getting an upfront payment for taking on a particular research project in exchange for giving up long-term licensing royalties. This explicit marriage between universities and corporations has the potential to take advantage of some of best research facilities in the world. The arguments for increasing the role of universities in research and innovation include the size of universities' research facilities, which outmatch those of most companies, and the universities' access to graduate students, who are some of the cheapest labor around. At places like MIT, engineering and business schools have worked together to think about new manufacturing processes, thus bringing universities further back to their industrial roots. These models do not explicitly involve philanthropy, although it seems likely that philanthropists would be interested in partnering to make such initiatives more beneficial for both parties.

## Ordinary People Needed (Who Need Opportunity)

If Benjamin Franklin, Oprah Winfrey, or Bill Gates had been born one thousand years earlier, what would they have been? Being born outside of the "court," they would have been ordinary people. They might have been peasant farmers or, at best, craftsmen. But none would have become an entrepreneur or a wealthy philanthropist. These options did not exist. For the purposes of this book, innovators, entrepreneurs, and philanthropists are ordinary people who were able to do extraordinary things because they had the opportunity. Many had modest beginnings, worked hard to make something of themselves, and later used their money to leave a lasting mark on society. They gave back to society, which had made them successful, thereby helping others to forge their own paths.

The mention of "ordinary people" brings us back to a central point of this book, which can get lost in all the talk about innovation and universities. American capitalism has been successful because it has balanced wealth creation with the extension of opportunity. Society has not walked this tightrope perfectly or without controversy, but it has held fast to a belief that individuals should have an equal chance at success *and* failure. As Jennifer Hochschild found in her study of individual attitudes toward inequality, both rich and poor Americans define "economic freedom as *an equal chance to become unequal.*"[10]

Today, universities are elite institutions. They can be expensive to attend, and expensive to get into because they require preparation and investment from parents. Some universities also carry an elite air of entitlement and superiority—consider the iconic images of eating clubs at Princeton University, the secret societies at Yale, and the final clubs at Harvard. Nonetheless, these universities are perhaps more meritocratic now than ever before, owing to waves of educational reformers and philanthropists who have made these particular schools practically free for students from middle-class families. Furthermore, much of the philanthropic giving to universities that isn't directed to research initiatives goes toward establishing merit-based scholarships, which work to expand the provision of mass opportunity.

Relatedly, one area where philanthropists have really turned up the heat is in supporting projects that transform elementary and secondary schools. In fact, foundation spending on such schools has surpassed that going to universities in recent years. Notably, the Gates Foundation spent $1.2 billion on K–12 education in the first half of the 2000s. No doubt, part of the reason for the aggregate shift in funding is the poor performance of grade-school education. Philanthropists rarely move alone, however, so much of the grantmaking has *followed* reformers—ending up in places like charter schools, Teach for America, and a diversity of other initiatives that have sought, among other things, to increase teacher pay, decrease the size of schools and classes, and create alternatives to public schools through vouchers. If anything, American philanthropy seems drawn to *new* ideas and rarely throws money at an old problem. This stinginess is a blessing and curse. Part of the entrepreneurial attitude among these funders is to support initiatives that won't just sustain the status quo but rather push against the grain.

Thus, philanthropists allocate money where they see potential for change. This was evident in the gift Mark Zuckerberg made to the Newark public school system, which was slated for an ambitious makeover under the star mayor Cory Booker. It was also evident when Alan Bersin, who was widely viewed as being capable of transforming the district, was put in charge of the San Diego public schools. When Bersin got the job in 1998, the San Diego school district was supported by about two million dollars a year in philanthropic contributions. Between 2000 and 2005, philanthropists gave the district more than fifty-three million dollars, which includes seven- and eight-digit gifts from foundations such as Gates, Hewlett, Broad, and Carnegie.[11]

## Why Philanthropy?

In order to understand American capitalism, it helps to have an appreciation for the role that philanthropy has played in strengthening its institutions. If politicians are going to forge policies that lead to steady, sustained growth, greater equality, and enhanced prosperity, philanthropy ought to be a key, if little-understood, factor. In many ways, it has been an invisible, underappreciated force for progress in American capitalism.

In terms of its overall size, philanthropy is pretty small, like a Band-Aid. Estimates vary, but it's likely that philanthropy makes up between $250 billion and $350 billion per year, which is around 3 percent of the U.S. economy. What's remarkable is that, as a share of GDP, philanthropy in the aggregate has been pretty steady for as long as there have been reliable data. Nonetheless, some still question whether philanthropic giving is large enough to make a difference. Compared to what the government spends overall on education, philanthropy's share is truly fractional.

Yet, what philanthropy has that government spending lacks is its almost singular focus on the aspirational, on looking in places and trying approaches that others have not or could not. Philanthropy is criticized for not being accountable, but this has also been part of its strength. Foundations can collectively shift billions of dollars with relatively little bureaucratic process required. Philanthropy is quick and innovative, and it understands creative destruction. Because it is tapped into networks of *reformers*, it can rapidly identify and correct shortcomings in the institutions of opportunity creation and innovation in America. Although this might suggest that philanthropy is driven by fads, such a conclusion would be unwarranted. Philanthropy has built the best universities in the world and some of the greatest centers of scientific research, and it has focused on finding cures for many diseases through its support of medical research. To discount these accomplishments as fads, or shortchange them as insignificant, would be utter denial.

## Is American-Style Capitalism Working?

We started this chapter with the question, "Is American-style capitalism working?" To answer that question we needed to be clear about what exactly American-style capitalism is. As Phil Auerswald and I wrote in a recent issue of *American Interest*, the essence of American-style capitalism is not a static Iron Triangle that balances the interests of large corporations and organized labor with the active intervention of government. Nor is it a rowdy free-for-all, where the interests of the many are readily subsumed to the acquisitive appetite of the few. Rather, American-style capitalism, as a Weberian ideal type, is a dynamic process by which opportunities create wealth that is in turn invested to create further opportunities. The success of American-style capitalism—the standard by which we judge it—must turn not on its transient ability to generate growth, but rather on its sustained ability to generate opportunity. However, taking action to support policies that promote opportunity is stymied by a political system that pits a party committed to economic liberty—the one with a historic affinity for free enterprise that today is handicapped by its 19th-century interpretation of the nature of markets and market failure—against a party committed to economic rights—the one

with a historical appreciation for the benefits that can de-
rive from enlightened government action but is today functionally handicapped by its 20th-century (Galbraithian)
interpretation of American-style capitalism. The result is a
depressing, ongoing stalemate in which neither side of the
aisle produces the policy initiatives required for renewed
prosperity.[12]

No wonder, then, that neither political party has produced an agenda to match the exigencies of the moment.
Republicans label as "corporate welfare" programs that
provide valuable support to technology entrepreneurs.
Democrats walk away from proposals to spur employment
by reducing the payroll tax. From both sides of the aisle
comes praise (explicit or implicit) for "shovel-ready" projects whose allure derives from the logic that the best way
to get out of a hole is to dig more deeply—and fast. The
outcome of our policy response to the Great Recession has
had at least one effect: it has sorted out who in Washington
is Keynesian and who isn't—in other words, who wants to
stimulate the economy and who instead wants to invent a
low-tax, low-regulation alternative.

As we discussed in chapter 2, the fundamental tension
in American-style capitalism is between encouraging vast
accumulations of wealth and keeping open the entryways
of economic opportunity. The strength of American-style
capitalism depends on the latter, so that upstart firms can
introduce innovations into the economy. When this works
well, however, a new challenge emerges: vast economic inequality, which threatens to undermine a different aspect of
opportunity, the ability to participate meaningfully in the
economy.

The market provides opportunity in the form of new
businesses, jobs and benefits, and goods and services—that

is, cheap goods. The story of affordable lighting told in chapter 3 suggested that cheaper goods can actually lead to a better life. In fact, the light bulb, even a single solitary bare light bulb, can make a huge difference in a person's life. Add to that the washing machine, refrigerator, bicycle, electric mixer, vacuum cleaner, automobile, television, computer, and cheaper food, and we can start to see that the market can improve our lives immensely. Nonetheless, cheap goods do not create opportunity. They make our lives better, but opportunity comes from somewhere else.

We are now in a better position to answer the question, "Is American-style capitalism working?" Three currents of American-style capitalism seem to be working fine: innovation, wealth creation, and philanthropy, although some would argue that we could us more innovation and philanthropy—especially more philanthropy. Today, one can easily answer that opportunity creation is not working as America struggles to dig itself out of the worst recession since the 1930s and our government is not focused on moving us in the right direction.[13] In fact, Joseph E. Stiglitz had the audacity to write, "America is no longer the land of opportunity."[14]

## The Estate Tax

What are the changes that need to be made to strengthen the relationship between entrepreneurship, philanthropy, and opportunity in America? This book has, thus far, not been about policy. My focus has not been on what should be done, but rather on describing the features of American capitalism and philanthropy. Nonetheless, if there is one policy that seems relevant to address—something that could actually strengthen the current system of capitalism—the estate tax would be that policy. The estate tax is perhaps the best mechanism available for creating incentives that move the wealthy toward philanthropy and away from idly holding on to their fortunes.

For the past ninety years, the United States has had some form of the estate tax, which has affected, on average, 2 percent of the population. At its peak in the postwar period, an individual with an estate valued at five million dollars or more would pay a 70 percent tax. In 2012, one with a fortune of about that size (more than $5.12 million) would pay a 35 percent tax. Anyone with an estate less than $5.12 million has no federal estate tax obligation in 2012 (rates and exemptions for future years have not been settled as I write this). The estate tax has been used both as a means of collecting government revenue and as a tool to limit the concentration of wealth. It's not surprising that the first estate tax was imposed during World War I, when the country needed revenue for the war effort and the Progressive movement, which opposed concentration of wealth, was nearing its peak. The initial estate tax was modest, but it established the basis for today's system of taxing large inheritances.

The estate tax is good for philanthropy because it has mostly permitted exemptions for charitable giving. Famously, in 1936, Henry Ford and his wife bequeathed most of their company stock to the newly created Ford Foundation instead of to their children. The move was viewed at the time as a blatant tax dodge, as Congress had recently hiked the estate tax to 70 percent on fortunes greater than fifty million dollars. The creation of their foundation saved the Ford family an estimated $321 million in taxes.[15] In practice, the estate tax nudges the wealthy to choose between becoming taxpayers or philanthropists. Some have chosen to just pay the tax or have worked assiduously to pay as little as possible, but many have created vast foundations with their wealth, completing the transformation from industrialist to philanthropist.

Nonetheless, despite the obvious importance of the estate tax in promoting philanthropy, many politicians and antitax advocates find the estate tax repugnant. They have misleadingly referred to it as the "death tax" in their efforts to rally public opinion against it, insinuating that it affects all taxpayers at their deaths, not just large estate holders. In part because of this antitax pressure, many conservative politicians, including President George W. Bush, advocated revoking or significantly decreasing the estate tax. In the tax cuts passed by the Bush administration in 2001 and 2003, for example, the estate tax was slated to gradually expire. Today, antitax ideologues still advocate continuing on this path.

I have argued that philanthropy is the invisible key to creating opportunity, entrepreneurship, and prosperity. More of it might indeed make for a better society. Perhaps we should try to raise the total amount from 2.5 percent of GDP to 3.5 percent—a 40 percent increase. Robert J. Shiller of Yale University proposes that we all think more about the ultimate purpose of our wealth: "There is a positive externality for all of us in seeing a society in which altruistic acts are common, and so governments should encourage such acts, even if the encouragement might be interpreted by some as appealing to selfish motives. There is often a fine line between selfishness and altruism, but a tax law that encourages people to accumulate wealth in order to gain recognition for giving it away should have the effect of promoting the general sense of a good society."[16] How to make it easier for more people to give away wealth becomes a public policy issue of the first importance. Shiller suggests that simplifying the tax code and using it to create incentives for philanthropy could increase giving.

Tax reform may not significantly affect the level of giving of individual wealthy donors but it does influence the way donations are made, particularly by corporations and philanthropic organizations such as foundations. A major study of high-net-worth philanthropy summarizes the history of foundations and tax legislation: "The relationship of foundations and Congress began with the Revenue Act of 1913, which exempted from taxation foundations and other organizations that operated exclusively for religious, charitable, scientific or educational purposes. In 1917, Congress allowed donors a charitable deduction for their contributions to such organizations, but passed no other legislation affecting them until the Revenue Act of 1943, which required foundations and certain other nonprofits to file an annual return listing income and expenses with the Internal Revenue Service."[17]

The Tax Reform Act of 1969 subjected foundations to taxation for the first time—a 4 percent excise tax on net investment income (later reduced to 2 percent)—and required foundations to distribute all their investment income within one year or award at least 6 percent of their assets in grants, whichever was greater. The 6 percent payout rate was later reduced to 5 percent.[18] The required minimum payout from foundations should be increased from the current 5 percent to 7 percent to accelerate opportunity creation.

The fundamental tension in American-style capitalism is between encouraging vast accumulations of wealth and keeping open the entryways of economic opportunity. If, as I have argued, what is wanting in the United States today is equal opportunity, then creating more opportunity should be an important public policy objective. With the wealth creation of the past decades we have a huge pool of wealth in this country. It should be put to good use sooner rather than later. Increasing the payout from foundations would put more resources to work at a time when the need is great. Although this might shorten the life of foundations, it may in fact be good public policy because we do not want foundations to last forever. More wealth will create new ones.

## Conclusion

In this chapter I have tried to explain what American-style capitalism is from the perspective of the currents of prosperity. American-style capitalism is neither European-style socialism, as the Right claims, nor is it a laissez-faire free-market economy, which the Left rejects. Rather, American-style capitalism, founded on liberal democracy, is a dynamic process in which opportunity creates wealth, which, in turn, is invested to create further opportunity. The current financial crisis and the deepening divide between rich and poor have called into question the future of capitalism. Many are asking the wrong questions because they do not understand the past. The United States today needs to create more opportunity—not just more entrepreneurship, but more innovative entrepreneurship. In order to do this, the United States needs to invest in ways that stimulate and expand the intersection of science, engineering, and entrepreneurship. We now turn to examining American-style capitalism in the global economy.

# CHAPTER 7

# THE GLOBAL PERSPECTIVE

For of those to whom much is given, much is required.
—JOHN F. KENNEDY

## America and the World

In this book, I have described American-style capitalism as interplay between innovators and entrepreneurs, on the one hand, and the vast system of universities, foundations, and research institutes they created, on the other hand. This back-and-forth has helped America navigate its dual obligation to create both wealth and opportunity—the critical balancing act that determines the true strength of a capitalist system. By opportunity, I mean the extent to which individuals can participate in the economic system, which is perhaps how the term is most commonly used, as well as the ability of new firms and new ideas to enter the economy.

As I wrote in chapter 1, philanthropy is the invisible, underappreciated force for progress in American-style capitalism—the secret ingredient that fails to get mentioned in economic accounts of capitalism. Philanthropy provides an extra gear, the fifth gear, that propels capitalism into overdrive. It is what gives American-style capitalism a competitive edge in the global economy. Including it gives us a fuller, more realistic picture of capitalism and therefore a better handle on how to govern it.[1]

At the heart of American-style capitalism is the largest system of knowledge-creating universities and research centers in the world, most of which are private and all of which have benefited from a vast allocation of philanthropic capital, which is itself tied to capitalism. Furthermore, foundations, developed during the nineteenth century explicitly to recycle wealth, have sustained and challenged existing ways of creating opportunity for millions of people, which is itself the fundamental benchmark by which capitalism should be judged.

American-style capitalism has contributed to the creation of opportunity much more than it is often given credit for. It is easy to point out that income inequality and persistent poverty in inner cities and rural areas have resulted from a heartless and individualistic system of capitalism—and maybe this is enough for some people to conclude that the American experiment is a failure—but this ignores the extent to which American capitalism has stayed true to opportunity creation throughout much of its history. The scope of philanthropy in America, even after controlling for the size of the U.S. economy, has been unmatched by any country at any time in history. Relatedly, the start-up rate of new firms and new ideas provides evidence of opportunity for upstarts and underdogs.

In the course of the book, chapters 2 through 5 worked though each of the four major currents of American-style capitalism: opportunity, entrepreneurship, wealth, and philanthropy. Chapter 6 brought these four currents together.

The purpose of this final chapter is to explore the American economy and American-style capitalism in the context of the global economy. Although the American experiment has survived and prospered for three hundred years, the system now faces new challenges both at home and abroad. Of course this is nothing new. Some have argued that our best days are behind us, but others have been more circumspect.[2] In this book I have suggested that American-style capitalism may be the only *sustainable* model for global development.[3] I have argued that what differentiates American-style capitalism from all other forms of capitalism is the opportunity it provides to challenge the status quo.

Does American-style capitalism offer the world a better path in the twenty-first century than communism did in the twentieth century? "Of course!" one might say. A more cautious answer, however, is: yes, but how does it do this? As I have argued throughout this book, American civilization is unique. In this final chapter, I revisit who we are, and then ask how we compare to the rest of the world, what our future looks like, and what the world will look like in 2050.[4] Finally, I ask whether the American model that is spreading around the world in bits and pieces could be better promoted.

## Who We Are

Early understanding of American exceptionalism was derived from the work of Alexis de Tocqueville, who wrote, "Democracy and socialism have nothing in common but one word, *equality*. But notice the difference: while democracy seeks equality in liberty, socialism seeks equality in restraint and servitude."[5] The descriptor *American exceptionalism* refers not to the embodiment of a superior domestic culture but to the idea that the United States is fundamentally different from any other nation.

As the Pulitzer Prize–winning author Gordon S. Wood writes, America is an *idea* about a country in which ordinary people are given extraordinary opportunities.[6] The ideal of equal opportunity suggests that all men and women are given an equal chance at the good life. Of course, this has never been true and is not true today. But America from its inception strove to provide equal opportunity for all; in fact, this ideal is proclaimed in the Declaration of Independence: "We hold these truths to be self-evident, that all men are created equal, that they are endowed by their Creator with certain unalienable rights, that among these are Life, Liberty and the pursuit of Happiness."

The case that America offers a different system of capitalism, a unique political economy, has been made perhaps most forcefully by Seymour Martin Lipset, the son of Russian immigrants and later an evangelist for American exceptionalism as a sociology professor at a number of prominent American universities. Lipset was fascinated with the United States, which he perceived as an outlier in many ways from other modern industrial countries. Later in life, he recognized Alexis de Tocqueville as one of his greatest influences, particularly as he sought to probe the foundations of what made America different. Lipset observed that the United States is the most "religious, optimistic, patriotic, rights-oriented and individualistic" country. America also has the lowest voter turnout rates among industrialized countries and yet the highest participation in voluntary organizations. Its provision of social welfare is very low and it has a rather blistering record of income inequality, but it is also incredibly meritocratic and upwardly mobile into professional and elite occupations.[7]

America's social characteristics are its egalitarian class structure and religious system, its focus on individualism,

and its weak central government. Its insistence on meritocracy results in a more productive economic climate, and its
strong emphasis on equal opportunity provides great motivation for individual success and social mobility. Americans
have never accepted the idea of a rigid hereditary class, and
hard work, ambition, education, and ability are considered
more important to success in life than social background.

The dominant religion in the United States is Protestant-
ism, which represents the epitome of bourgeois values, including hard work and frugality. (The bourgeoisie is the social class between the aristocracy, or very wealthy, and the
working class or proletariat.) In the Protestant ethic, making money is acceptable, but money cannot be allowed to
fray the social fabric. In other words, individuals are free to
accumulate wealth, but that wealth must be invested back
into society to maintain and expand opportunity.

America and its political institutions are unique. Although pieces of the institutional structure exist in other
countries, it is most fully developed in America. Some countries offer opportunity. Some countries allow their citizens
to create great wealth. But in many places that occasionally
boast of rapid rates of growth, such as Indonesia and Rus-
sia, institutionalized giving is almost unknown. Capitalist
growth expands because it creates wealth. The majority
of wealth generates economic opportunity through investments that seek the maximum private return. Opportunity
encourages entrepreneurial effort. This is a good thing. But
it in turn concentrates wealth, which may act in its own
service to perpetuate inequality.

In many ways it seems as though the United States is the
unofficial leader in opportunity, entrepreneurship, wealth
creation, and philanthropy. Although some countries might
arguably do better in one of these categories than the United

States at some point in time, it seems uncontroversial to say that the United States has packaged this as a model more than any other country has.

## America, Europe, and East Asia

Let us compare three models of liberal democracy—the East Asian democracies, the members of the European Union, and the United States—in terms of opportunity, entrepreneurship, wealth, and philanthropy. These successful models of liberal democracy have similar economic and political systems, in the sense that they are all capitalist countries run by democratic governments, but they have different institutional structures. East Asia has a strong state, America has a weak state, and Europe is in between.

East Asia's development model places a high priority on the relationship between government and business, as the state plays an important role in business development. In East Asian countries, in general, governments create economic opportunities, direct investment, and drive growth. In Japan during the 1980s, so the story goes, brilliant bureaucrats led industry after industry to conquer global markets. The East Asian model led to high levels of process innovation and wealth creation. *Largely because of the strong tradition of the state*, however, the philanthropic sector in East Asia is very small or nonexistent. Thus the model works very well for replicating ideas and exploiting knowledge created elsewhere, but the strong state kills individual initiative and does not lead to breakthrough innovations.

European capitalism lies somewhere between East Asian capitalism and American-style capitalism. In many respects Europe is still seen as the Old World, which is why people have been moving from Europe to the United States for centuries in search of opportunities that Europe did not provide. For a start, Europe has less opportunity for entrepreneurship. All the data bear this out, whether you look at the start-up rate of high-tech firms, the number of companies going public, or the number of high-profile entrepreneurs. Because there are fewer entrepreneurs in Europe, there is also less new wealth.

In response to the information technology revolution (chapter 3), a few years ago the British government launched a program to encourage more people to become entrepreneurs. In essence, the government wanted the British to become more like Americans. Arguably, there are more entrepreneurs in America than in Britain, and many more people from Britain move to America to become entrepreneurs than the reverse, because America gives middle-class people the opportunity to succeed. In fact, this has been true for four centuries! Great Britain has accounted for 10 percent of high-tech immigrant entrepreneurs in the United States in the past decade. Conversely, almost no Americans have gone to Britain to become high-tech entrepreneurs. The obvious question is, why not? The answer is that the United States is set up to grow businesses and the United Kingdom is less so.

Of course, there is some entrepreneurship in Europe, just not an entrepreneurial economy. SAP is one of the best examples of high-tech entrepreneurship in Europe. It was started in the 1970s by five former IBM engineers who had a great idea for software. They tried to raise money from German banks for a business venture. As the story goes, the German banks told them that since they worked at IBM, if the idea were any good then IBM would do it. Such are the critical trappings of a managed economy that I highlighted

in chapter 3. The opportunity for new wealth creation—
for decentralized innovation that the American university
model has perfected—was lacking in Germany at the time.
The entrepreneurs were funded by a small regional bank.
Today, SAP ranks ninety-first on the *Financial Times*'s list
of the five hundred largest global companies, just behind
Siemens, BASF, and Daimler. It has annual sales of seventy-
five billion dollars and employs fifty-four thousand people
worldwide.[8]

There has also been an ideological backlash against
philanthropy in Germany and other countries in Europe.
Much of the resistance is to private and voluntary initiatives taking over the role of the state. Peter Kraemer, a German multimillionaire, has been highly critical of the Giving
Pledge. When Gates and Buffett went to Germany to try
to convince billionaires there to sign the pledge, they were
rejected. Nonetheless, many of these billionaires had given
much of their money away.

For example, Dietmar Hopp, one of the cofounders
of SAP, has transferred about 70 percent of his wealth to
his foundation, which focuses on education and health research, yet he did not sign the Giving Pledge. Similarly, two
other cofounders of SAP, Hasso Plattner and Klaus Tschira,
have established private foundations and are active in philanthropy. Why exactly they did not sign the Giving Pledge
is unclear, but clearly these three seem to fit the model of
philanthropy and entrepreneurship.

One reason that philanthropy is less robust in European
countries than in the United States is that these countries
have strong social welfare systems—much stronger than
that in the United States—and therefore Europeans feel as
though opportunity is adequately provided by the state. As
I've argued in this book, however, state-run social welfare

institutions are usually for helping those who cannot take advantage of the capitalist system, but they rarely have the ability to revitalize and nurture those who are actively engaged, as the American university system has done, for example, in promoting opportunity—in the form of change and redevelopment of the systems of knowledge creation, research, and commercialization.

According to Yves Beigbeder, a French author and lawyer who spent many years at the World Health Organization, "In contrast to the American philanthropic tradition of altruism for the common good and of American private aid to global causes for the benefit of poor countries, the French socialist state is to blame; the welfare state that neglects, suspects, or rejects the private efforts of philanthropy or of 'charity'; the 'public' must do everything, the 'private' must deal with neither health nor education, associations must deal with the burden of cumbersome procedures."[9]

One way to think about American-style capitalism and other countries is to think of liberal market economies versus coordinated market economies. The United States is an example of a liberal market economy, along with Australia, Canada, and the United Kingdom. Coordinated market economies include Germany, Japan, the Netherlands, France, Denmark, and Italy. These two types of economies differ along two crucial dimensions. First, the coordinated market economies have more coordinated employment protection and lower stock market valuations. In other words, they protect workers more and therefore also have less wealth. Liberal market economies, such as the United States, have much less employment protection but create more wealth. Why is this so?

A crucial difference between these two types of economies is found in the types of innovations they pursue. The

United States focuses on cutting-edge innovations that start new industries. In the United States, Microsoft as a start-up was not unusual in its ambition to create a new industry (software for personal computers)—though of course its success has been far beyond the scope of all but a small handful of other entrepreneurial ventures. In Germany, by contrast, SAP was an outlier in creating a whole new industry (integrated enterprise management software). So Americans focus on radical innovations that bring about new industries, whereas Germans focus on making their existing products better. Just think of a new BMW! So the United States needs less employment protection to create more wealth, and Germany needs better workers to make better cars.

We see this when we look at the types of patents that German and American inventors apply for. Germans specialize in civil engineering, mechanics, machine tools, surfaces, and materials. Americans specialize in basic materials, agriculture, biotechnology, control systems, optics, telecommunications, and semiconductors. In other words, the United States focuses on inventing the future while Germany focuses on perfecting the present. The U.S. system demands weak employment protection and vigorous entrepreneurship, and it leads to greater wealth. Or, to revisit Schumpeter, it practices more creative destruction.

For this reason, American-style capitalism needs to recycle wealth and has relied on philanthropy for that function. It also keeps up investments in education and knowledge creation that are vital for radical innovation. The Germans do not.

In addition to submitting to the forces of creative destruction, American-style capitalism differs from coordinated market economies in a second critical way. America's focus on wealth creation has been accompanied by innovations in methods of recycling wealth. Both of these stem from American views of individualism, agency, and human nature. Other countries do not recycle money through the private sector. But in other countries there is also much less opportunity to make lots of money. As a result, Europe has fewer entrepreneurs, more security, more charity, and less philanthropy—and therefore less opportunity for innovation.

## The World in 2050

In a now-classic essay published in the late 1980s, Francis Fukuyama wrote that the triumph of the West was evident in the total exhaustion of viable systematic alternatives to Western liberalism. He was writing as the Soviet and Eastern European system was collapsing and the triumph of Western liberal democracy seemed inevitable. He used the phrase *the end of history* to signify "the end point of mankind's ideological evolution and the universalization of Western liberal democracy as the final form of human government."[10] The end of history turned out not to be the long-predicted convergence of capitalism and socialism but rather a clear victory of economic and political liberalism.

In many ways, it seems as though the end of history has not yet been written; within liberal democracies, there are still fundamental choices that define the way in which societies deal with wealth—both its creation and its diffusion back into society. When the United States was making its tectonic shift from a managerial economy to one that was more entrepreneurial (discussed in chapter 3), the basic foundations of liberal democracy remained, but the relationship between government and business changed dramatically, along with the innovative potential of the American economy and the vitality of creative destruction. In a global sense, the innovative and entrepreneurial system of the United States is distinct, as is the extent to which voluntary and philanthropic forces work with and around government to shape the foundation of American opportunity.

A second Gilded Age began at the close of the twentieth century and has yet to run its course. The great foundation of this current cycle is barely ten years old and has yet to make its full potential felt. The Gates Foundation, like the Carnegie Corporation and the Rockefeller Foundation, may need fifty years for the tremendous good it is doing for society to be fully appreciated. Meanwhile, some of the wealthier of this second Gilded Age have not become philanthropists yet. What might Mark Zuckerberg accomplish in his life if he becomes a true philanthropist? Clearly, we are facing a critical time in our history. As we search for ways to secure our future, the underlying values of our republic should be our guide. We need to reinforce our commitment to opportunity, innovation, wealth creation, and philanthropy.

What does the next decade look like? As we stare into the abyss of financial crisis, global recession, population explosion, and mounting ecological challenges, many are asking what the human prospect is in the next few decades. The abyss looks so bleak because we are staring into it with the wrong lens. The lens is farsighted, giving our leaders a distorted view of the U.S. economy, which makes it difficult to take action.

As we peer into the twenty-first century, it is clear that the world is at the dawn of a great rebuilding. Whereas the

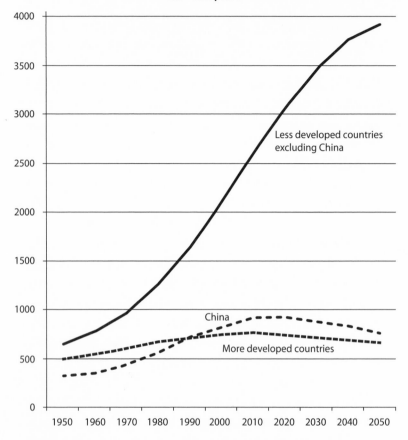

**Figure 4**. Labor Force (Population Age 15–59), in 000,000s, UN 2009 Medium Variant Projection
*Source:* Zoltan J. Acs and Laszlo Szerb, *Global Entrepreneurship and Development Index* (Cheltenham, UK: Edward Elgar, 2012), vi.

financial crisis will pass—they always do—the world still faces two great sustainability challenges. The first is figuring out the institutional structure of liberal democracy in a globalized world with a rapidly increasing population. By 2050, the world population will increase by three billion people, most of them in the developing world. As shown in figure 4, the labor force in the developed world will decline and the developing world will have to take up the entrepreneurial challenge. Entrepreneurship is a young person's game. In other words, innovation and entrepreneurship will have to come more from developing countries. I call this the *social sustainability* challenge.

As Richard Florida suggests, removal of trade barriers and capital flows creates efficient markets, but the results are what economists call a Zipf distribution: a few big winners and lots of losers—economic opportunity tends to concentrate and losers become frustrated. Turning for consolation to religious fanaticism or some substitute becomes the default.[11] This is true in both the developed and developing worlds. Marx and Keynes knew this and suggested that institutions needed to be rigged. They both advocated eliminating or at least constraining the entrepreneur and private wealth.

There are three broad approaches to social sustainability: (1) lift the losers above some minimum level of mass consumption (illusions of fame trump economics); (2) restore order (ram it down their throats) at home and abroad; or (3) create structures that enable full use of people's talent, self-expression, and entrepreneurship—in a nutshell, that create opportunity for all. *The United States could do more good for the global economy by showing the world how to create opportunity than by any other single act.* Yet perhaps we are failing at the very thing we were once good at. America was the first country to get it right and it may be the first country to get it wrong.[12] By *get it right* I mean that the United States developed a set of institutions to create equality of opportunity for most. By *get it wrong* I mean that we now have a set of institutions that may not be creating opportunity for most. The argument has been made perhaps most strongly by Joseph E. Stiglitz: "I have seen the picture in many developing countries; economists have even given it a name, a dual economy, two societies living side by side, but hardly knowing each other, hardly imagining what life is like for the other. Whether we will fall to the depths of some countries, where the gates grow higher and the societies split farther and farther apart, I do not know. It is, however, the nightmare toward which we are slowly marching."[13]

As Lawrence Summers, the former president of Harvard University, writes and this book argues, "Perhaps the focus needs to shift from inequality in outcomes, where attitudes divide sharply and there are limits to what can be done, to inequalities in opportunity. It is hard to see who could disagree with the aspiration to equalise opportunity or fail to recognise the manifest inequalities in opportunity today."[14]

The second great challenge is *ecological sustainability*. For years we have been talking about global warming, with many conflicting views and differing ideological positions. Meanwhile, the evidence seems to be mounting that average global temperatures are rising, the polar ice caps are melting, and weather patterns are becoming more erratic. The result will be wide-scale flooding, spreading desserts, and increased human suffering.[15] Sustainability typically requires and facilitates a truly eclectic multidisciplinary approach. This makes traditional universities perhaps unsuitable to provide the breeding ground for "sustainability science." If we could go back to the drawing board, one would want to build multidisciplinary research clusters around scientists and build multidisciplinary research teams around pieces of the puzzle. Whole universities could be set up around these issues globally, just as Carnegie, Duke, and Stanford did more than a century ago.

These two sustainability challenges are linked, for the more we create social sustainability—opportunity for all—

the easier it will be to find solutions to our environmental problems through entrepreneurship and innovation. These twin sustainability challenges, like slavery in the nineteenth century and the creation of a broad middle class (suffrage, civil rights, and human rights) in the twentieth century, need to be addressed. The success of American-style capitalism in the twenty-first century will be judged not at the beginning of the century, not in ten years, but far down the road. The real question is not what the future of America holds but rather what the future of humankind will look like.

## Can the Model Be Exported to Other Countries?

In the age of globalization, most observations about political economy have been on the theme of convergence, the idea that the world is moving toward one dominant system à la Fukuyama's *The End of History* or Thomas Friedman's *The World Is Flat*. It seems strange to think of the United States as having a different model. Nonetheless, American-style capitalism is fundamentally different from the style of capitalism practiced in the rest of the world. To be sure, the postwar system of U.S. capitalism of the 1950s through the early 1970s looked similar to a West European model, in which the government played a much more active role in the economy and a few large firms dominated each industry.

The entrepreneurial revolution changed all of that. Why is there so much entrepreneurship in the United States? Or why is there not a similar amount in the rest of the world? The answer, as I have argued in this book, has to do with how American institutions are uniquely set up to facilitate the creation of new wealth through bringing radical innovations to market. This process begins with inventions and patents—something that many developed countries do well—but then relies on the ability to turn these inventions into business plans, requiring investment and faith that the new business will not be squeezed out through regulation or collusion among existing firms in the market.

Interestingly, however, American entrepreneurship thrives not just because the United States is better at innovating than other countries, but also because it is so good at incubating inventions when they are in their developmental stage. The number of patents has been fairly steady in the United States, Western Europe, and Japan since the 1960s, but the United States tends to exploit these patents at a higher rate, commercializing them and turning them into businesses.

As we saw in chapter 3, innovating entrepreneurs who creatively disrupt the system are the norm in an entrepreneurial economy. What has made this possible again in the United States? It was a profound change in values, attitudes, and above all behavior. It is the application of a new "technology" to the economy. Following the entrepreneurial revolution in America, in 1985 Peter Drucker wrote: "It is still too early to say whether the entrepreneurial economy will remain primarily an American phenomenon or whether it will emerge in other industrially developed countries. . . . . So far, the entrepreneurial economy is purely an American phenomenon."[16] Although Drucker thought that entrepreneurial capitalism might emerge in Japan, it did not. Japan is a rich, slow-growing economy manufacturing cars and computers.

David Audretsch and Carl Schramm both describe in detail the economy of the 1950s, carefully documenting the interaction among labor, big business, and government. They describe the tipping point during the years of transition in the United States and come to similar conclusions about the nature of American-style capitalism. They do not see its future in the same way, however.

Audretsch believes that the rest of the world learned from the American model, thereby threatening America's comparative advantage. He notes, "America had in ten years transformed itself from a self-doubting society to one of self-celebration. America had it, and the rest of the world did not. . . . . Having spent considerable time in Europe and Asia observing recent efforts to create their versions of an entrepreneurial society, I wondered, 'What will the United States do when the rest of the world catches up?' "[17]

Carl Schramm has an answer for Audretsch. Far from fearing an entrepreneurial transformation around the globe, the future of the American experiment actually depends on the rest of the word emulating it. Schramm writes: "For the United States to continue its global leadership, it must help the world see clearly the breadth and depth of our economic evolution. . . . . It is in Americans' interest to see our system replicated all over the world. We must believe that in flourishing entrepreneurial economies the widening distribution of wealth and the creation of new jobs will naturally help lead to the spread of democracy. . . . . *It is imperative that we—everyone everywhere—go into this entrepreneurial future together.*"[18]

The question, however, is: What type of capitalism? Not the good versus bad types that I mentioned in chapter 1, but a system that is built on radical innovation and philanthropy or one that is built around coordinated market economies? Or, to put it differently, will every country in the world follow the German and Japanese model of innovation? Or will some countries try to build an American-style capitalism?

This book has argued that it is philanthropy, not entrepreneurship, that propels the basic machinery of American-style capitalism. So in addition to well-functioning markets, property rights, contract law, capital markets, and the like, philanthropy—a little-understood economic force—provides a superinstitutional element that serves to promote vital nonmonetary institutional forces (university research) necessary for achieving growth through technological innovation, promoting economic equality, and cultivating economic security. This feedback loop has helped America fulfill its dual obligation to create both wealth and opportunity—the critical balancing act that determines the true strength of a capitalist system.

The fact that this distinctive force appeared in America is important, but the greater point here is that it serves as a model for countries around the world *with more inflexible capitalist institutions*. It is, of course, tempting to argue that the interplay between entrepreneurship and philanthropy is just another case of American exceptionalism, but what this means is unclear. America's relationship with entrepreneurship has been uneven, despite entrepreneurship being critically important in much of the country's early development.

What we now know is that this system—what I've called American-style capitalism—has germinated in other countries, whether or not it is welcomed with open arms. This American style of capitalism is showing its head in other countries and challenging the traditional relationship between states. How do we think about this? Even in the United States, the dominant interpretations of capitalism have not considered these intersections and interdependencies of entrepreneurial business and entrepreneurial capitalism.

Evidence for the spread of American-style capitalism is found in both entrepreneurship and philanthropy. Of the nineteen most generous billionaires, those who have given away at least one billion dollars, thirteen are from the United States. The others are from Switzerland, Germany, India, Mexico, and Hong Kong. This leads to three observations. First, all but one, Stephen Schnidheiny, are self-made—entrepreneurship is alive and well. Second, thirteen of the nineteen are Americans, although only 45 percent of billionaires are from America. Third, they are all focused on building opportunity. Patrick Soon Shiong, MD, is focusing his efforts on building a health-care information highway, for example.[19]

If the six hundred billionaires outside the Unites States could find a philanthropic means of investing their billions in research (à la American philanthropy) they could change their countries and the world for the better. This book thus makes the case for a larger global culture of philanthropy. Today, more than half of the billionaires in the world live outside the United States but only two non-Americans have signed the Giving Pledge. The data show that outside the United States, philanthropy has lagged behind.

The reason is clear. Li Ka-shing said in a 2006 speech, "In Asia, our traditional values encourage and even demand that wealth and means pass through lineage. . . . I urge and hope to persuade you that if we are in a position to do so, that we transcend this traditional belief. . . . Even if our government structure is not yet geared towards supporting a culture of giving, we must in our hearts see building society as a duty in line with supporting our children."[20]

The two non-U.S. signatories of the Giving Pledge are both Asian. Vincent Tan, born in 1952, is the chairman and CEO of Berjaya Corporation Berhad, which controls a wide array of businesses. In 2010 he made the *Forbes* billionaire list with an estimated worth of $1.3 billion. Born in

Batu Pahat, Johor, in Malaysia, Tan worked as a clerk and an insurance agent before going into business in the 1980s. In 1982 he purchased Malaysia's McDonald's franchise, and in 1985 he bought the lottery agency Sports Toto when it was privatized by the government. On April 14, 2011, he pledged to donate at least half of his wealth to charity through the Giving Pledge campaign.

China's best-known philanthropist, Chen Guangbiao, has become the first of his country's moguls to commit to giving away his money in response to Gates and Buffett's Giving Pledge. Guangbiao pledged to leave his estimated $440 million fortune to charity upon his death.[21]

Ahn Cheol-Soo, a software entrepreneur in South Korea, is starting a foundation worth $195 million to address issues of income inequality in his own country. This contribution will make Ahn Cheol-Soo one of the biggest philanthropists in South Korea, a country with virtually no history of philanthropy despite having more than one-third the number of billionaires per capita as the United States, as shown in figure 3 (in chapter 5).

Even Europe, which shares many Western values with America, has a very low level of philanthropy despite having a considerable wealthy elite as measured by the number of billionaires per capita. Of course, the entrepreneurship-philanthropy nexus, an American invention born out of liberal democracy and a free market, cannot be easily integrated in those parts of the world where these values are not shared.

Although philanthropy is almost nonexistent outside of America, charity does play an important role, especially in India and the Middle East. Charity in these regions takes a very traditional form: looking after the poor. Therefore, the Gates Foundation's influence seems to be limited outside of the United States. In India, for example, with its significant charity sector, the Gates initiative has had almost no impact. Nonetheless, it has started a discussion about the moral duty of the wealthy to give back and has led to a call for more moral models.

## Conclusion

What does the world need now? Many, especially in the United States but also globally, argue that the world needs more entrepreneurship and innovation. True, we could use more innovation to solve lots of problems. But we need more innovative entrepreneurship and less replicative entrepreneurship.

Nonetheless, I am not so sure that this is our greatest need. We have just had an information revolution that spread around the world like wildfire. Today, four billion people, or 60 percent of the population of the world, have cell phones.[22] Never before has a technology spread to so many so fast and so far. Perhaps what the currents of American prosperity suggest is that what the world needs now, and in the immediate future, is more opportunity—and that means more philanthropy. At this point in the development of humankind, we are on the cusp of truly being able to grasp the future. *So to create opportunity for many, what we need today is much more philanthropy and less charity in the world at large.* This is what will secure our collective future.

As former President Clinton pointed out (see chapter 1), the world today faces problems that government alone will not be able to solve. Many of the problems are global and will need global solutions. Already, thousands of nonprofit organizations, funded by philanthropic contributions and government money alike, are solving global issues of poverty and disease. This back-and-forth between entrepreneurship and philanthropy will help the world navigate its dual obligation to create both wealth and opportunity—the critical balancing act that determines the true strength of a capitalist system.

Whether some countries will follow the American example remains an open question. Although American money is focused in part on global issues, much more needs to be done in the world. If the six hundred billionaires outside the United States engaged in philanthropy—which means creating opportunity for individuals to meet the demands of this economy—we could start to create the social and ecological sustainability that will be needed in this century. So what should global money do? The history of American-style capitalism suggests that we create opportunity, innovation, wealth, and philanthropy. How did we do this?

America provided education for the middle class and tied it to local economic development, so one thing we can learn from three centuries of the American experiment is that building great research universities is an investment that pays great dividends down the road. Just think what a Carnegie Mellon or a Stanford University would mean to the future of any developing country. If Carlos Slim, the wealthiest person in Mexico, would endow a world-class research university in Mexico—one that could compete with academic talent from all over the world—consider the transformative effect this could have on innovation and R&D in Mexico.

American-style capitalism, with its interplay between entrepreneurship and philanthropy, on the one hand, and its balancing act between wealth and opportunity, on the other, should be encouraged despite the unequal distribution of wealth entrepreneurship creates, because historically, much of the new wealth created has been given back to the community to build institutions that have had a positive effect on future economic growth. Rather than the government constraining the rich through taxes, the rich can campaign for social change by creating opportunity. For example, the fight against slavery had some very wealthy backers, as did the creation of our great universities. If we shut off the opportunities for wealthy individuals to accumulate wealth and then give it back, we will also shut off the creation of wealth, which has far greater consequences for an entrepreneurial society.

What is required to sustain American-style capitalism into the twenty-first century? A global philanthropic revolution![23] Through philanthropy, the unequal distribution of wealth can be channeled into creating opportunity for future generations through creating knowledge today. Sustaining global capitalism will require vision and investment from billionaires all over the world. If the new rich rise to the occasion, then prosperity will continue well into this century as the coming golden age of philanthropy creates the investments that lead to positive feedback loops of opportunity, innovation, and future prosperity.

# EPILOGUE

## CHANGING THE TAX LAWS

In every wise struggle for human betterment one of the main
objects, and often the only object, has been to achieve in large
measure equality of opportunity.

—THEODORE ROOSEVELT

A few years ago, my family and I were on vacation in
southern France. One evening after dinner in Saint-Tropez,
a small crowd had gathered at the harbor. The crowd was
swarming around a brand-new yellow Ferrari. Why all the
fuss? In this playground of the rich and famous, another
luxury car was nothing to get excited about. But it was not
the car that created the excitement—it was the message.
Written on the windshield in brilliant red lipstick was the
message, "Bobby, on your 18th birthday, Love, Mother."

This book has made the argument that the indiscriminate use of income for personal consumption is bad for
society, as is the use of wealth for maintaining a class structure. In the past few years, the rich have embarked on a
cringe-inducing orgy of spending. For example, a limited-
edition Prada crocodile handbag sells for forty-one thousand dollars, not much less than the median U.S. family
annual income.[1]

Robert Frank suggests that the way to deal with the first issue—indiscriminate use of income for personal consumption—is to institute a progressive consumption tax.[2] It's not a sales or value-added tax. Neither of those takes individual income into account. Individuals would report their income and annual savings. The tax would be based on taxable consumption, such as the $350,000 Ferrari in Saint-Tropez, as opposed to savings that would lead to growth and investment. Luxury spending is context dependent; we all want to "keep up with the Joneses." If we were all Calvinists, no one would spend more on consumption than their neighbors. But we are not, and individual and social interests do not always coincide, as Keynes reminded us. So it would be helpful to use tax incentives to nudge us toward investments that would benefit society and away from ostentatious personal consumption that would not.

A progressive consumption tax has been supported by both the Right and the Left. Even Milton Friedman suggested in a 1943 article that a progressive consumption tax is the best way to reduce conspicuous consumption and encourage investment.[3] All those interested in avoiding the consumption tax would increase their investment. Warren Buffett would go even further. He would levy higher taxes on the rich. He would like to see people who earn their money from investing pay more than those who earn it through labor. He would also tax speculative gains at a much higher rate and put the directors and CEOs of publicly bailed-out companies on the hook for their net worth if their companies fail.[4]

Our second issue is the use of wealth to maintain a class structure. On this, the Right and the Left do not always agree. Although the two issues are related (conspicuous consumption is practiced by the rich), their solutions are

different. Here we need to deal with *wealth*, not *income*.
Nobody likes the estate tax. Why should half of your parents' property revert to the state upon their deaths? It's stu-
pid! You work hard to leave your children something, and
half of it evaporates. But that is not really the issue. The estate tax is not about the family farm; it is about American-
style capitalism. As Tocqueville wrote, "What is most important for democracy is not that great fortunes should not
exist, but that great fortunes should not remain in the same
hands. In that way there are rich men, but they do not form
a class."[5]

In 2001, Milton Friedman advocated repealing the estate
tax: "Spend your money on riotous living—no tax; leave
your money to your children—the tax collector gets paid
first. That is the message sent by the estate tax. It is a bad
message and the estate tax is a bad tax. The basic argument
against the estate tax is moral. It taxes virtue—living fru-
gally and accumulating wealth."[6] When he was the deputy
secretary of the treasury, Lawrence H. Summers expressed a
very different view, as reported in the *Washington Post*: " 'In
terms of substantive arguments,' the evidence put forth by
lawmakers advocating repeal of the estate tax 'is about as
bad as it gets. . . . . When it comes to the estate tax, there is
no case other than selfishness.' "[7] The second Bush administration worked to reduce the estate tax. Although many ap-
plauded this move, others recognized that the tax serves an
important function in our pluralistic society. So why do we
need an estate tax? The answer is not what you might think.

In this book I have argued that what differentiates
American-style capitalism from all other forms of capitalism is its historical focus on both the creation of wealth
(entrepreneurship) and the reconstitution of wealth (philanthropy). Philanthropy remains part of an implicit social

contract stipulating that wealth, beyond a certain point, should revert to society.

Individuals are free to accumulate wealth; however, that wealth must be invested back into society to expand opportunity. In this sense, the United States was a new type of nation, the product of a shift in human character and social roles. This new character type possessed unprecedented powers of discretion and self-reliance, yet was bound to collective ends by novel forms of institutional authority and internal restraint. Historically, much of the new wealth created in the United States has been given back to the community to build up the social institutions that enhance future economic growth. Though it is widely recognized that the great nineteenth-century philanthropists laid the foundation for later wealth creation and social stability, this has not been quantified or placed within the framework of private and public costs and benefits.

Today, however, the value of giving back is not universally shared, even in the United States, where the rich have retreated from the challenge of recycling their wealth to maximize the benefit to society. What is required to sustain U.S. and global capitalism in the twenty-first century is a renewed spirit of philanthropy among the new rich, which will set an example for the rest of the world. Sustaining global capitalism will require vision and investment from Americans and dissemination of the ideas that make U.S. capitalism successful.

More than one hundred years ago, Andrew Carnegie put philanthropy at the heart of his Gospel of Wealth. For Carnegie, the question was not only how to gain wealth but, equally important, what to do with it. He suggested that billionaires, instead of bequeathing vast fortunes to their heirs or making benevolent grants in their wills, should administer their wealth as a public trust during their lifetimes. Wealth over a hundred million dollars, and certainly over a billion dollars, should revert to society through philanthropy, not taxes. The estate tax, Carnegie argued, is an insurance policy that preserves the very foundation of our great pluralistic society.[8]

Without the estate tax, American philanthropy will likely persevere, as it did before the tax was imposed. As this book has demonstrated, there appears to be something endemic in the history and culture of American capitalism that sustains philanthropic giving. Thus, the tax is hardly a necessary condition for generosity, and many of the signatories of the Giving Pledge would probably move forward with their philanthropic goals with or without it. At a time when America is as dependent as ever on reinvigorating its economic and social health, however, it would seem foolish to risk undercutting philanthropy, which has been wedded to promoting opportunity creation and innovation throughout American history.

# PLEDGE LETTERS

Why does someone give away a billion dollars? It is a fascinating question. And why they do it today is even more fascinating than looking at why someone did it one hundred years ago. We can better relate to our own times. The individuals who have signed the giving pledge have each written a letter explaining why they have chosen to give their money away. All ninety-one letters can be found on the giving pledge website (http://givingpledge.org) and are worth reading. I have studied all of these letters and they have played an indispensable role in my research. Here I have reproduced, with permission, some of the letters. I include the letters from Bill and Melinda Gates and Warren Buffett because of the important role they played in the pledge. I also include the letters from David Rockefeller (old money) and Michael Milken (new money), and three of the most interesting letters, from David Rubenstein, George Kaiser, and Peter Peterson: men of humble beginnings who thought that giving away their money was the right thing to do.

## Bill Gates and Warren Buffett

March 4, 2009

Mr. David Rockefeller
30 Rockefeller Plaza; Room 5600
New York, New York 10112

Dear David:

The two of us have been talking a lot about our experiences with philanthropy. We thought it would be good to get together a group of about a dozen like-minded people around one table to broaden the discussion. Our goal would be to share perspectives and discuss whether there is more we can all do to support and encourage others who have not yet reached the same stage.

We both admire the collaborative spirit that you and your family have brought to philanthropy. So we wanted to come to you first, to see if you would be interested in hosting this discussion with us. We would want to have the meeting in New York, and while Bill is going to be out of the country for most of the next three months we both have a calendar window on May 5 that we are hopeful might work for you.

Thank you for your consideration. Bill would like to call you tomorrow or Friday to discuss this with you.

Sincerely,

*Bill Gates*
*Warren Buffett*

# Warren Buffett

*My Philanthropic Pledge*

In 2006, I made a commitment to gradually give all of my Berkshire Hathaway stock to philanthropic foundations. I couldn't be happier with that decision.

Now, Bill and Melinda Gates and I are asking hundreds of rich Americans to pledge at least 50% of their wealth to charity. So I think it is fitting that I reiterate my intentions and explain the thinking that lies behind them.

First, my pledge: More than 99% of my wealth will go to philanthropy during my lifetime or at death. Measured by dollars, this commitment is large. In a comparative sense, though, many individuals give more to others every day.

Millions of people who regularly contribute to churches, schools, and other organizations thereby relinquish the use of funds that would otherwise benefit their own families. The dollars these people drop into a collection plate or give to United Way mean forgone movies, dinners out, or other personal pleasures. In contrast, my family and I will give up nothing we need or want by fulfilling this 99% pledge.

Moreover, this pledge does not leave me contributing the most precious asset, which is *time*. Many people, including—I'm proud to say—my three children, give extensively of their own time and talents to help others. Gifts of this kind often prove far more valuable than money. A struggling child, befriended and nurtured by a caring mentor, receives a gift whose value far exceeds what can be bestowed by a check. My sister, Doris, extends significant person-to-person help daily. I've done little of this.

What I can do, however, is to take a pile of Berkshire Hathaway stock certificates—"claim checks" that when converted to cash can command far-ranging resources—and commit them to benefit others who, through the luck of the draw, have received the short straws in life. To date about 20% of my shares have been distributed (including shares given by my late wife, Susan Buffett). I will continue to annually distribute about 4% of the shares I retain. At the latest, the proceeds from all of my Berkshire shares will be expended for philanthropic purposes by 10 years after my estate is settled. Nothing will go to endowments; I want the money spent on current needs.

This pledge will leave my lifestyle untouched and that of my children as well. They have already received significant sums for their personal use and will receive more in the future. They live comfortable and productive lives. And I will continue to live in a manner that gives me everything that I could possibly want in life.

Some material things make my life more enjoyable; many, however, would not. I like having an expensive private plane, but owning a half-dozen homes would be a burden. Too often, a vast collection of possessions ends up possessing its owner. The asset I most value, aside from health, is interesting, diverse, and long-standing friends.

My wealth has come from a combination of living in America, some lucky genes, and compound interest. Both my children and I won what I call the ovarian lottery. (For starters, the odds against my 1930 birth taking place in the U.S. were at least 30 to 1. My being male and white also removed huge obstacles that a majority of Americans then faced.)

My luck was accentuated by my living in a market system that sometimes produces distorted results, though overall it serves our country well. I've worked in an economy that rewards someone who saves the lives of others on a battlefield with a medal, rewards a great teacher with thank-you notes from parents, but rewards those who can detect the mispricing of securities with sums reaching into the billions. In short, fate's distribution of long straws is wildly capricious.

The reaction of my family and me to our extraordinary good fortune is not guilt, but rather gratitude. Were we to use more than 1% of my claim checks on ourselves, neither our happiness nor our well-being would be enhanced. In contrast, that remaining 99% can have a huge effect on the health and welfare of others. That reality sets an obvious course for me and my family: Keep all we can conceivably need and distribute the rest to society, for its needs. My pledge starts us down that course.

## Bill and Melinda Gates

Parents all over the world do their best to give their children great opportunities. They work to give their children every chance to pursue their own dreams.

However for too many parents, their dreams of giving their families better lives are dashed. In the United States, their children don't get the education they need to succeed in life. In the developing world, their children succumb to diseases that have long since been eradicated in rich countries.

Years ago, when we began to learn about global health, we were especially shocked to read that one highly preventable disease— rotavirus—was killing half a million children every year. Airplane crashes are always front-page news, yet here was a killer of half a million children every year, and most people couldn't put a name to it, much less put a stop to it.

We have committed the vast majority of our assets to the Bill & Melinda Gates Foundation to help stop preventable deaths such as these, and to tear down other barriers to health and education that prevent people from making the very most of their lives. Our animating principle is that all lives have equal value.

Put another way, it means that we believe every child deserves the chance to grow up, to dream and do big things.

We have been blessed with good fortune beyond our wildest expectations, and we are profoundly grateful. But just as these gifts are great, so we feel a great responsibility to use them well. That is why we are so pleased to join in making an explicit commitment to the Giving Pledge.

The idea of the pledge came out of discussions we had with other givers about what they were doing, about what had worked in philanthropy and what had not worked. Everyone shared how giving had made their lives richer. Everyone who attended was inspired by listening to the others' passion and encouraged to do even more.

For the two of us, because we see amazing progress every day, but also, how much more work remains, we're honored to be a part of this pledge effort.

For example, to us, vaccines are miracles, tiny vessels of hope and promise. And the world has made progress in vaccinating millions of children. But there are still millions more who die of preventable diseases.

So we want to make sure lifesaving vaccines reach everyone who needs them, and that the world develops new vaccines.

We've seen similar progress in America's education system. We have visited schools that are breaking down old barriers and preparing every child for college and life. These are great schools—but there are not nearly enough of them. Now the task is to make sure that every student gets the same opportunity to succeed in college and in life.

Both of us were fortunate to grow up with parents who taught us some tremendously important values. Work hard. Show respect. Have a sense of humor. And if life happens to bless you with talent or treasure, you have a responsibility to use those gifts as well and as wisely as you possibly can. Now we hope to pass this example on to our own children.

We feel very lucky to have the chance to work together in giving back the resources we are stewards of. By joining the Giving Pledge effort, we're certain our giving will be more effective because of the time we will spend with this group. We look forward to sharing what a wonderful experience this has been for us and learning from the experience of others.

Best wishes,

*Bill and Melinda Gates*

## George B. Kaiser

July 26, 2010

Post Office Box 21468
Tulsa, Oklahoma 74121-1468
(918) 491-4501

I suppose I arrived at my charitable commitment largely through guilt. I recognized early on, that my good fortune was not due to superior personal character or initiative so much as it was to dumb luck. I was blessed to be born in an advanced society with caring parents. So, I had the advantage of both genetics (winning the "ovarian lottery") and upbringing. As I looked around at those who did not have these advantages, it became clear to me that I had a moral obligation to direct my resources to help right that balance.

America's "social contract" is equal opportunity. It is the most fundamental principle in our founding documents and it is what originally distinguished us from the old Europe. Yet, we have failed in achieving that seminal goal; in fact, we have lost ground in recent years. Another distinctly American principle is a shared partnership between the public and private sectors to foster the public good. So, if the democratically-directed public sector is shirking, to some degree, its responsibility to level the playing field, more of that role must shift to the private sector.

As I addressed my charitable purposes, all of this seemed pretty clear: I was only peripherally responsible for my own good fortune; I was morally duty bound to help those left behind by the accident of birth; America's root principle was equal opportunity but we were far from achieving it. Then I had to drill down to identify the charitable purposes most likely to right that wrong.

The discoveries of stem cell research and brain development in recent years provided some guidance for me. Though almost all of us grew up believing in the concept of equal opportunity, most of us simultaneously carried the unspoken and inconsistent "dirty little secret" that genetics drove much of accomplishment so that equality was not achievable. What the new research seemed to suggest, however, was that brain cells were functionally unformed at birth and that only through the communication among them—driven by trial and error interpretation of sensory stimulation shortly after birth—did our cognitive and social/emotional skills develop. As I sometimes joke, I remember vividly that place before birth as being warm, wet, dark . . . and boring. Then, suddenly, as I emerged, I was bombarded with sensory overload and had to interpret all of that strange stimulus. Most of that interpretation takes place by age three; after that, we can modify our destiny but it is a lot harder.

No child is responsible for the circumstances of her birth and should not be punished for it in this life. (I will leave the question of second chances to other pulpits.) I have therefore developed my charitable focus around the concept of providing the greatest opportunity for self-fulfillment for each child, focusing on those who arrive in the least advantaged circumstances. (A purer focus would be in areas of much greater disadvantage in the world where fewer dollars accomplish more. I honor the Bill & Melinda Gates Foundation's commitment to the principle that "every life has equal value" but will leave my justification for a primarily American focus to another dissertation.) That governing concept has led us to those initiatives which attempt to reverse the generational cycle of poverty, especially for very young children and their families: prenatal healthcare; early learning and development for at-risk kids, birth to three; family healthcare; parenting training; job and income assistance for families with young children; operating a robust program to provide alternatives to incarceration for mothers who have committed non-violent crimes, etcetera.

These efforts focus most heavily on the causes of poverty but we also dedicate resources to the symptoms, especially in these difficult times and in our relatively poor part of the country— food, clothing, shelter, healthcare and civic projects that promote inclusiveness and vibrancy. We generate a mix of projects, some of which are leading edge and more that import best practices from the greater creativity and experience of others. We attempt to leverage other resources, public and private, by our example. We try not to let a budget drive our expenditures but rather pursue those efforts through which we can make a true difference at an appropriate cost, whether less than or more than our targeted allocation. We remain lean in our central organization and partner with the leading practitioners in our fields of endeavor. We tend to direct our purposes and carefully monitor targeted results on a contemporaneous basis rather than scattering gifts and trusting to retrospective general narratives of success from the beneficiaries. All in all, it is an intoxicating and yet frustrating journey, led by an extraordinarily committed and talented cadre of leaders.

Now that I have told you far more than you wanted to know about how I arrived at my charitable commitment and direction, it is time to make the pledge: I am entranced by Warren's and Bill's visionary appeal to those who have accumulated unconscionable resources, to dedicate at least half of them back to purposes more useful than dynastic perpetuation. My family is very well provided for and they join me in my intention to devote virtually all of my financial resources to the same general charitable purposes I have pursued in life, better informed in specifics by our experience and the experience of others. If enough acolytes follow Bill's and Warren's example, then maybe we will more closely approach the ideal of equal opportunity throughout the United States and the world.

*George B. Kaiser*

## Michael and Lori Milken

December 2010

Dear Warren, Bill and Melinda,

We've long embraced the principles of *The Giving Pledge*. Charity is something we learned at an early age, whether during grade school riding our bikes around the neighborhood collecting dimes and quarters for the American Cancer Society, or later, participating in community service programs in high school. From the time we began formal philanthropic programs in the 1970s, we've made contributions at a rate that will assure distribution of the overwhelming majority of assets during our lifetimes.

The charitable programs we began when we were in our early 30s to advance education and progress against life-threatening diseases were later formalized with the launch of our family foundations in 1982. Our goal has been to discover and advance inventive and effective ways of helping people help themselves and those around them to lead productive and satisfying lives. We do that primarily through our work in education and medical research.

In education, our focus has been on seeking out, recognizing and rewarding exceptional teachers and developing programs that can help America regain the educational leadership it once enjoyed among nations. In medical research, we've been committed to advancing basic and applied science, but also to supporting healthcare programs to assure the well-being of all community members. The challenges in both these areas were and remain immediate, which made it clear to us that we should act immediately rather than wait decades to establish a legacy.

Charitable involvement has taught us many lessons:

- The kind of world in which our children and grandchildren reach their potential depends on the success of our efforts to provide opportunities for all children.
- Whether in education or medical research, early funding of promising young talent generates a lot more progress than handing out lifetime-achievement awards.
- The most-effective programs create an environment that brings people in disparate organizations and disciplines together—industry, academic and government researchers, for example—to accelerate the process of discovery.
- Philanthropy is far more than just writing checks. It takes an entrepreneurial approach that seeks out best practices and empowers people to change the world.

- Follow your passion. We believe philanthropists should begin the process of giving by asking what they care about passionately. Intensely felt core beliefs provide the motivation to stick with a project through successful completion.

Although it has been our privilege to be able to provide financial support for a wide range of programs, we believe it's just as important to donate time and transfer knowledge, not just money. The effect of large gifts is magnified when the giver contributes skills. There's no substitute for rolling up your sleeves and working with the people who can make a difference. They get the benefit of your participation and you gain a direct understanding of the real problems and potential solutions, which makes you a more informed giver.

Thank you for the opportunity to make this pledge.

Sincerely,

*Michael Milken      Lori A. Milken*

### Peter G. Peterson

June 17, 2010

Mr. Warren E. Buffett
Chairman
Berkshire Hathaway Inc.
Omaha, NE 68131

Dear Warren:

I am very pleased to pledge that I plan to contribute the substantial majority of my assets to philanthropy. As you know, I am well on my way.

I do so with great pleasure. And for several reasons.

My parents were Greek immigrants who came to America at age 17, with 3rd grade educations, not a word of English and hardly a penny in their pockets. Their dream was the American dream, not just for themselves but for their children as well.

My father took a job no one else would take—washing dishes in a steamy caboose on the Union Pacific railroad. He ate and slept there and saved virtually every penny he made. He took those savings and started the inevitable Greek restaurant, open 24 hours a day for 365 days a year for 25 years. Throughout this period, he always sent money to his desperately poor family in Greece and fed countless numbers of hungry poor who came knocking on the back door of his restaurant. Above all else, he wanted to save so as to invest in his children's education.

As I watched and learned from my father's example, I noticed how much pleasure his giving to others gave him. Indeed, today, I get much more pleasure giving money to what I consider worthwhile causes than making the money in the first place. As I checked with other philanthropists, I found this was a very common experience.

For example, I have been particularly pleased to support causes and institutions for which I have a passion and for which I contribute myself, that is my personal capital, as well as my financial capital. For example, the Peterson Institute for International Economics, the Council on Foreign Relations and The Concord Coalition that I co-founded with Senators Warren Rudman and Paul Tsongas.

I was also informed by the great novelist, Kurt Vonnegut, who once told a story that seemed to capture my situation perfectly. He and Joseph Heller were at a party given by a wealthy hedge fund manager at his majestic beach house in the Hamptons, the summer playground on Long Island where the rich and famous congregate. Kurt and Joe both had made their marks by satirizing life's absurdities—Kurt with best-selling novels like *Slaughterhouse 5* and *Breakfast of Champions*, Joe with the incomparable *Catch-22*. During the course of the party, Kurt looked around at the surroundings and asked Heller: "Joe, doesn't it bother you that this guy makes more in a day than you ever made from the worldwide sales of *Catch-22*?" Joe thought for a moment and then said, "No, not really. I have something that he doesn't have." "What could you possibly have that he doesn't have?" Kurt asked. "I know the meaning of enough." My father often said the same thing.

When I enjoyed a most surprising billion dollar plus windfall from the public offering of The Blackstone Group, a firm I co-founded, I pondered, what should I do with all of this money?

In 2007, I decided I already had far more than enough and was delighted to commit a billion dollars to the Peter G. Peterson Foundation and to some causes that I care deeply about.

My foundation made its first major contribution to a transcendent global threat, the proliferation of nuclear weapons. I have known former Senator Sam Nunn, for whom I have enormous respect, who is devoting much of his life to this cause.

I am also much concerned about domestic threats that I also consider transcendent. I refer to several such threats as undeniable, unsustainable and yet, politically speaking, untouchable. For example, our unfunded entitlement promises that so many depend upon, our ballooning debts to foreign lenders, which combined with our very low savings, leaves us very vulnerable and even threaten our national sovereignty. Then, of course, there are our mushrooming healthcare costs that threaten to bankrupt our economy.

We, at the Foundation, are deeply involved in educating, motivating and, hopefully, activating the public to do something about these problems.

I am a very lucky American dreamer but I want to see that dream alive for my five children's and nine grandchildren's generations. On our current path, I fear we are imperiling their future by passing on massive, hidden debts and unthinkable taxes. At bottom, I consider this fiscal child abuse or mortgaging their future, or whatever one chooses to call it, it is not only an economic issue but a national security issue and, above all, a moral issue.

Given the serious political challenges and our country's apparent reluctance to accept the required shared sacrifice, no doubt many are saying my Foundation is not only a presumptuous mission, but a foolhardy one. So, I quote my old University of Chicago professor George Stigler, "If you have no alternative, you have no problem." I asked myself this melancholy question: How will I feel 10 to 20 years from now if I look back and ask why, oh why did we all leave such a legacy? How could we have done this, not simply to America, but to our own children and grandchildren? Could there be a worse feeling? Can *not* trying really be an acceptable alternative?

Finally, Warren, you and Bill Gates know better than anyone how distinctly American private philanthropy is.

I thank you warmly and congratulate you and Bill Gates mightily for your leadership role in this most worthwhile cause.

Best,

*Peter G. Peterson*


# David Rockefeller


*Philanthropic Pledge*
July 21, 2010

Philanthropists, at their best, try to address serious societal problems and occasionally come up with innovations that lead to enduring change. In the end, success requires much more than financial resources, although money is, of course, essential Good ideas are just as important; otherwise one risks wasting both the funds and the opportunity. Effective philanthropy also requires patience - patience to deal with unexpected obstacles; patience to wait for the first, slight stirrings of change; and patience to listen to the insights and· ideas of others.

For five generations, my family has experienced the real satisfaction and pleasure of philanthropy. Our engagement has helped to create a strong group of institutions, including the University of Chicago, The Rockefeller University, the Museum of Modern Art, and the Rockefeller Brothers Fund. The practice of philanthropy also has enabled many of us to become personally involved in efforts to address critical global challenges such as poverty, health, sustainable development, and environmental degradation. Our family continues to be united in the belief that those who have benefitted the most from our nation's economic system have a special responsibility to give back to our society in meaningful ways.

Warren Buffett and Bill and Melinda Gates share this belief and have challenged others to pledge half their assets to philanthropy during their lifetime or at their death. I am pleased to say this has long been my intent and my practice, and I am delighted to have been asked to participate in this important initiative. I hope that others will accept this challenge—and opportunity— and will join us in this worthwhile endeavor.

I also hope that our efforts to expand the scope of philanthropy as individuals, in collaboration with others, and in ways that include not only financial resources but innovative ideas and patience, will be part of the gift we all bequeath to the future.

*David Rockefeller*

# David Rubenstein

*Pledge*

Like many of those who responded positively—and enthusiastically—to Bill Gates' and Warren Buffett's call, I never expected, in my wildest dreams as a youth or as a young professional, to be in a position where anyone (other than my immediate family) would care what I would do with my money. That is because I did not expect to have much of it. I also did not see wealth accumulation as a likely professional outcome, or even a particularly desirable one.

I was born and raised in modest, blue collar circumstances in Baltimore. The making of large sums of money—and the disposition of them—was just not on my radar screen.

My goal was simply to do well enough in school to secure scholarships to college and law school to practice law; and to fulfill a long-time desire—perhaps inspired by President Kennedy's inaugural address—to move back and forth from the practice of law into various public service positions. And I was on that course—I graduated from the University of Chicago Law School—with the assistance of considerable scholarship money—practiced law in New York at Paul, Weiss, Rifkind, Wharton & Garrison—and (through luck far more than skill) managed three years after law school to find myself as a deputy domestic policy assistant to President Carter.

I expected that I would stay at the White House for eight years—the voters obviously felt four years of my service was enough—and would then live a life of shuttling back and forth into government service from a Washington law firm perch, with the goal of hopefully doing some public good during each time in government service. The income level of a Washington lawyer does not allow for the accumulation of large wealth, but I felt it was more than enough to satisfy my somewhat Spartan needs and the likely needs of any family I would produce and raise.

And then, as is the case with so many individuals who accumulate wealth, my life did not go in the direction I had expected or intended, or desired. After a few years of practicing law following my White House days, I realized that I was not all that great a lawyer; I had growing reservations about constantly uprooting my career to go back and forth into government, (especially as a family emerged); and I felt that I should try to do something I might enjoy more than law or government service.

And so I started a small investment firm in Washington—a rarity for the city in the late 1980's. My original partners and I struggled to raise the first $5 million to capitalize the firm, and we spent many years trying to get investors and others to take us seriously—an experience not uncommon to most entrepreneurs in their early years.

But, nearly a quarter century later, this tiny firm grew to be one of the world's largest private equity firms, producing for the founders and many others in the firm more wealth than we had ever expected or dreamed about.

In my own case, I had been relatively tunnel-visioned in trying to build the firm, and spent little time on philanthropic matters until I turned 54. I then read that a white male, on average, would live to 81, meaning that I had already lived, if I were to match the average, two thirds of my life. I then thought that I did not want to live the other third, get to my deathbed, and then ask someone to give away my accumulated resources as they saw fit (even if I left some guidance in a will). I also thought that my resources had become—and would likely be at death—far more than my family reasonably needed.

So I decided to put my toe into the world of philanthropy, and did get reasonably involved from that point forward. My approach in the ensuing seven years has not been as systematic as may be desired. I have begun to contribute to a wide variety of performing arts, educational, medical, literary, public service, and cultural causes and institutions—causes that have meaning to me, and institutions that were very helpful to me earlier in my life or I think are now being very helpful to others. I now serve on a few dozen non-profit boards—far too many to focus one's philanthropic interests. But I enjoy these boards and the causes and the purposes for which they serve.

However, I recognize that to have any significant impact on an organization or a cause, one must concentrate resources, and make transformative gifts—and to be involved in making certain those gifts actually transform in a positive way. And I am heading in that direction, and hope—if I do get to 81—to have made many such transformative gifts by that time. And, with luck, some of them may actually have transformative benefits - hopefully during my lifetime - for the organization or the cause.

In signing the Pledge, I did not honestly do anything more than I had already intended to do, as I said to Bill Gates when he talked to me about the Pledge. I actually had already made arrangements to ensure that a good deal more than half of my resources would have gone to philanthropic purposes

So in participating in the Pledge, I cannot honestly say that I am now committing to do more than what I had been planning to do for some time, and was in the process of doing. But I felt that the Pledge was a quite positive undertaking, and was pleased— and honored—to be asked to be part of it, for these reasons:

1) To the extent that individuals with considerable resources are publicly committing to give away at least half of their wealth, other individuals with considerable wealth in this country may be inspired to do so as well—and that would be a positive

development, especially if the individuals had not previously thought about or felt obligated to give away that much.

2) To the extent that the publicity surrounding the Pledge affects other Americans, it is my hope that it will inspire individuals with resources of modest or average or even above average means to make similar pledges—to themselves, their families, or to the public. The giving away of money should not be seen as only an obligation—or as a pleasure—restricted to the wealthiest (and most fortunate) among us. Everyone can and should give, and everyone can and should feel that their gifts may make the world a little bit better place. And if every person with the ability to make some philanthropic gifts does so, the country will be much better for these gifts, and the donor will surely feel much better about himself or herself.

3) Philanthropic activity is, unfortunately, more of an American phenomenon than a global phenomenon. My hope is that the Pledge will inspire similar efforts to get under way abroad. And while it is likely such efforts will focus on the wealthiest of individuals in other countries, my hope, again, is that individuals of all levels of resources will also increase their giving, and feel they are helping their countries and humanity by doing so.

In my own case, I would add as a final point, one a bit beyond what the Pledge seeks. I hope to do my own giving—and to honor my Pledge—while I am alive. I recognize no one really knows how long he or she will be on the earth, and it is therefore difficult if not impossible to time one's giving perfectly to match one's longevity. But I enjoy seeing the benefits—when they arise—of my giving, and would like to have as much of this enjoyment while I am alive as possible.

I recognize that others signing the Pledge—now or in the future—may have a different perspective, and their considerable resources (or age) may make the goal of honoring the Pledge during their lifetime a bit less realistic. But I do hope that others involved in this effort—and those who are ultimately inspired to increase their giving—will accelerate their giving, so as to bring whatever benefits come from giving to the world a bit sooner. That can only make the world a bit better a bit sooner. Too, watching the product of one's giving is one of life's greatest pleasures, and those with the ability to do so should do what they can to experience that pleasure when they are around to see the benefits. They will never regret doing so.

# NOTES

## Chapter 1
## A Conversation

1. http://online.wsj.com/article/SB10001424052748704017904575
409193790337162.html.
2. http://givingpledge.org/#george_lucas.
3. http://givingpledge.org/#paul+g.+_allen.
4. http://givingpledge.org/#pierre+_omidyar.
5. *USA Today*, 12 August 2010.
6. http://blogs.wsj.com/wealth/2010/10/15/
worlds-richest-man-charity-doesnt-solve-anything/.
7. The British, in their own version of the Giving Pledge,
pledge to give 10 percent to charity. Not much has changed in old
Europe. http://www.forbes.com/sites/seankilachand/2012/01/18/
british-elite-support-their-own-giving-pledge/.
8. Robert J. Shiller, *Finance and the Good Society* (Princeton, NJ:
Princeton University Press, 2012), chapter 18.
9. Richard Posner, *A Failure of Capitalism: The Crisis of '08 and
the Descent into Depression* (Cambridge, MA: Harvard University
Press, 2009).
10. William Baumol, Robert Litan, and Carl Schramm, *Good Capitalism, Bad Capitalism, and the Economics of Growth and Prosperity*
(New Haven, CT: Yale University Press, 2007).
11. Francis Fukuyama, "The End of History?" *The National Interest*, Summer 1989, 3–18.
12. "Les Miserables," *The Economist*, 28 July 2012.
13. Zoltan J. Acs and Laszlo Szerb, *The Global Entrepreneurship
and Development Index* (Cheltenham, UK: Edward Elgar, 2012).
14. Olivier Zunz, *Philanthropy in America: A History* (Princeton,
NJ: Princeton University Press, 2012).

15. Ibid.

16. Bill Clinton, "Charity Needs Capitalism to Solve the World's Problems," *Financial Times*, 20 January 2012.

17. Zoltan J. Acs and Ronnie Phillips, "Entrepreneurship and Philanthropy in American Capitalism," *Small Business Economics* 19 (2002): 189–204.

18. Douglass C. North, *Institutions, Institutional Change and Economic Performance* (Cambridge: Cambridge University Press, 1990).

19. Rana Foroohar, "Warren Buffett Is on a Radical Track," *Time*, 23 January 2012, 34.

20. http://www.goodreads.com/author/quotes/98221. Robert_F_Kennedy.

21. E. J. Dionne Jr., "Romney's Type of Capitalism," *Washington Post*, 12 January 2012, A17.

22. Philip Auerswald and Zoltan J. Acs, "Defining Prosperity," *The American Interest*, May/June 2009, 4–13.

## Chapter 2
## Creating Opportunity

1. Jared Diamond, *Guns, Germs, and Steel: The Fates of Human Societies* (New York: W. W. Norton, 2005); John Maynard Keynes, "Economic Possibilities for Our Grandchildren," in *Essays in Persuasion* (New York: W. W. Norton, 1963).

2. Joseph A. Schumpeter, *Capitalism, Socialism and Democracy* (New York: Harper and Bros., 1942).

3. David Brooks, "The Hamilton Agenda," *International Herald Tribune*, 9–10 June 2007, 9.

4. John R. Thelin, *A History of American Higher Education* (Baltimore: Johns Hopkins University Press, 2004).

5. Frederick Rudolph, *The American College and University: A History* (Athens: University of Georgia Press, 1990).

6. Ibid., 32.

7. Ibid., 33.

8. Ibid., 248.

9. Thelin, *A History of American Higher Education*.

10. Christopher Lucas, *American Higher Education: A History* (New York: St. Martin's Press, 1994), 147.

11. Merle E. Curti and Vernon Carstensen, *The University of Wisconsin: A History, 1848–1925*, volume 1 (Madison: University of Wisconsin Press, 1949).

12. Ibid., 87.

13. Quoted in ibid., 88.

14. http://givingpledge.org/#tashia+and+john+_morgridge.

15. Kenneth Sokoloff and Stanley Engerman, "History Lessons: Institutions, Factor Endowments, and Paths of Development in the New World," *Journal of Economic Perspectives* 14, no. 3 (2000): 217–232.

16. Ibid.

17. David Hackett Fischer, *Albion's Seed: Four British Folkways in America* (New York: Oxford University Press, 1989).

18. Bill Gates speech, National Education Summit on High Schools, Washington, DC, 26 February 2005.

19. John E. Chubb and Terry M. Moe, *Politics, Markets, and America's Schools* (Washington, DC: Brookings Institution Press, 1990).

20. Olivier Zunz, *Philanthropy in America: A History* (Princeton, NJ: Princeton University Press, 2012), 178.

21. Ibid., chapter 6.

22. Robert T. Grimm Jr., ed., *Notable American Philanthropists* (Westport, CT: Greenwood, 2002), 116.

23. *Vidal v. Girard's Executors*, 43 U.S. 127 (1844).

24. Frederick M. Hess, *The Future of Educational Entrepreneurship: Possibilities for School Reform* (Cambridge, MA: Harvard University Press, 2008), 96.

25. http://books.google.com/books?id=RExYAAAAYAAJ&pg
=PA11102&lpg=PA11102&dq=To+help+an+inefficient,+ill
-located,+unnecessary+school+is+a+waste.+%E2%80%A6&source
=bl&ots=Kr_nwTD_l6&sig=JXspVHw5luB6P_aJvdG3bbSxAk&hl
=en&sa=X&ei=DkgYULTCGsreoQGh5YE4&ved=0CD4Q6AEw
AQ#v=onepage&q=To%20help%20an%20inefficient%2C%20
ill-located%2C%20unnecessary%20school%20is%20a%20
waste.%20%E2%80%A6&f=false.

26. Tyler Cowen, *The Great Stagnation* (New York: Dutton, 2012).

27. http://www.insidehighered.com/news/2012/05/08/walmart-and
-american-public-u-chart-new-ground-partnership#.T6lT1nUV9_E
.email.

28. Lawrence Summers, "How the Land of Opportunity Can Combat Inequality," *Financial Times*, 16 July 2012, 15.

## Chapter 3
## Entrepreneurship and Innovation

1. According to the eighteenth-century mathematician and philosopher Jean Le Rond d'Alembert, "The universe would only be one fact and one great truth for whomever knew how to embrace it from a single point of view." In *The Information: A History, a Theory, a Flood* (New York: Pantheon, 2011), James Gleick argues that information is more than just the content of our libraries. It is "the blood and fuel, the vital principle" of the world. If information is the key to understanding everything, then information technology is the key to making that understanding a reality. As cited in "Are We No More Than All These Bits?" *International Herald Tribune*, 19–20 March 2011, 20.

2. Ray Allen Billington and Martin Ridge, *Westward Expansion: A History of the American Frontier* (New York: Macmillan, 1982).

3. Quoted in Ralph E. Gomory, "Learning Outside the Classroom: The Time Is Now," in *Conference Proceedings, Second International ALN Conference* (1996), 1. http://www.google.com/url?sa=t&rct=j &q=&esrc=s&frm=1&source=web&cd=1&sqi=2&ved=0CDEQFjAA &url=http%3A%2F%2Fsloanconsortium.org%2Fconference%2Fpro ceedings%2F1996%2Fdoc%2F96_gomory.doc&ei=10EYUIzBHuPdo QGY8ICYBw&usg=AFQjCNFoLemQi9Eyk9gAbUOrJ6194Oj8Lw.

4. http://en.wikipedia.org/wiki/Andrew_Carnegie.

5. http://en.wikipedia.org/wiki/Thomas_Edison.

6. Mark Dodgson and David Gann, *Innovation: A Very Short Introduction* (Oxford: Oxford University Press, 2010).

7. Ibid.

8. http://en.wikipedia.org/wiki/Bell_Labs.

9. http://en.wikipedia.org/wiki/Sputnik_1.

10. Robert F. Hébert and Albert N. Link, *The Entrepreneur: Mainstream Views and Radical Critiques* (New York: Praeger, 1988), 43.

11. Joseph A. Schumpeter, *Capitalism, Socialism and Democracy* (New York: Harper and Bros., 1942), 134.

12. Quoted in Robert B. Reich, *Supercapitalism: The Transformation of Business, Democracy, and Everyday Life* (New York: Alfred A Knopf, 2007), 27.

13. John Maynard Keynes, *Essays in Persuasion* (New York: W. W. Norton, 1963), 313.

14. Reich, *Supercapitalism*, 29.

15. Karl Marx, *Capital*, trans. Ernest Untermann (Chicago: Kerr, 1925–1926), 1:836.

16. Tim Wu, *The Master Switch: The Rise and Fall of Information Empires* (New York: Alfred A. Knopf, 2010).

17. Robert D. Putnam, *Bowling Alone: The Collapse and Revival of American Community* (New York: Simon and Schuster, 2000), 88.

18. Norman Macrae, "The Coming Entrepreneurial Revolution: A Survey," *Economist*, 25 December 1976, 42.

19. George Harris, "The Post-capitalist Executive: An Interview with Peter F. Drucker," *Harvard Business Review*, May–June 1993, 115–116.

20. Clyde H. Farnsworth, "U.S. Industry Seeking to Restore Competitive Vitality to Products," *New York Times*, 18 August 1980, A1.

21. Agis Salpukas, "Depressed Industrial Heartland Stressing Urgent Need for Help," *New York Times*, 19 August 1980, 1.

22. Peter J. Schoyten, "Amid Stagnation, High Technology Lights a Path," *New York Times*, 20 August 1980, A1.

23. Henry Scott Stokes, "Can Japan's Aid to Its Industry Guide U.S.?" *New York Times*, 21 August 1980, D1.

24. Edward Cowan, "Carter Economic Renewal Plan," *New York Times*, 22 August 1980, D1.

25. David B. Audretsch, *The Entrepreneurial Society* (Oxford: Oxford University Press, 2007), 89.

26. Modern information technology begins with the invention of the transistor, a semiconductor device that acts as an electric switch and encodes information in binary form (0,1). The first transistor was constructed at Bell Labs in 1947, for which John Bardeen, William Shockley, and Walter Brattain won the Nobel Prize in Physics in 1956. The transistor replaced the vacuum tube in computers and televisions and gave us the transistor radio. The next major milestone in information technology was the coinvention of the integrated circuit by Jack Kirby of Texas Instruments in 1958 and Robert Noyce of Fairchild Semiconductor in 1959. Before the invention of the integrated circuit we did not have handheld calculators. The third invention was the microprocessor, in 1973, which incorporated the central processing unit (CPU) on a single integrated circuit. The technological leap was the 4004 computer chip. The first commercially available microprocessor was produced by Intel Corporation. The sale of Intel's 8086-8088 microprocessor to IBM in 1978 for incorporation into the PC was a major business breakthrough for Intel.

27. http://en.wikipedia.org/wiki/Michael_Dell.

28. But what sparked this revolution? Surely the turbulence of the 1960s, a cultural revolution, played an important role in transforming America from a world of the "organization man," in which "father knows best," to a world in which experimentation and innovation again dominated American life.

29. Zoltan J. Acs and David B. Audretsch, *Innovation and Small Firms* (Cambridge, MA: MIT Press, 1990).

30. The rise in IPOs was probably due mainly to institutional reforms that lowered taxes on capital gains and allowed institutional investors such as pension funds to invest in venture capital firms. This made it possible for mature privately held firms to go public.

31. http://www.cato.org/publications/commentary/remembering-ronald-reagan.

32. As important as Bayh-Dole was, it was essentially an attempt to "reverse engineer" the technology transfer process that had worked so effectively in prior years at a few very special institutions such as MIT and Caltech. The Research Corporation for Science Advancement, established in 1912, played an important role in commercializing research results at several leading academic institutions. In response to the incentives offered by Bayh-Dole, a wide range of universities adapted to the new set of rules and began promoting technology transfer, but the vast majority of them never developed the kind of permissive, entrepreneurial culture that marked the early models.

33. Zoltan J. Acs, Bo Carlsson, and Charlie Karlsson, eds., *Entrepreneurship, Small and Medium-Sized Enterprises and the Macroeconomy* (Cambridge: Cambridge University Press, 1999), chapter 8.

34. *Wall Street Journal*, 2 March 1993.

35. Macrae, "The Coming Entrepreneurial Revolution."

36. The rankings of leading firms in the United States are constantly changing.

37. "The Knowledge Factory: A Survey of Universities," *The Economist*, 4 October 1997.

38. Steve Allen, "Microsoft's Odd Couple," *Vanity Fair*, May 2011.

39. Ibid.

40. Zoltan J. Acs, *Innovation and the Growth of Cities* (Cheltenham, UK: Edward Elgar, 2002), chapter 1.

41. Sarah Rimer, "A Hometown Feels Less Like Home," *New York Times*, 6 March 1996, 1.

## Chapter 4
## The Wealth of Nations

1. "Times Higher Education World University Rankings, 2011–12," http://www.timeshighereducation.co.uk/world-university-rankings/.
2. *Business Week*, 25 August 1997, 66.
3. http://www.stanford.edu/dept/visitorinfo/basics/about.html.
4. http://en.wikipedia.org/wiki/List_of_colleges_and_universities_in_the_United_States_by_endowment.
5. Joyce Appleby, *The Relentless Revolution* (New York: W. W. Norton, 2010), 23.
6. John Maynard Keynes, *Essays in Persuasion* (New York: W. W. Norton, 1963), 369.
7. Timothy Noah, "The United States of Inequality," *Slate*, 16 September 2010, http://www.slate.com/id/2266025/entry/2266816/.
8. http://givingpledge.org/#herb+and+marion+_sandler.
9. The Center on Philanthropy at Indiana University, *Bank of America Study of High Net-Worth Philanthropy—Initial Report*, October 2006.
10. Thomas J. Tierney, "Higher-Impact Philanthropy: Applying Business Principles to Philanthropic Strategies," *Philanthropy*, 14 February 2007. http://www.philanthropyroundtable.org/article.asp?article=1453&cat=147.
11. Franklin Parker, *George Peabody: A Biography* (Nashville: Vanderbilt University Press, 1971), 208.
12. http://givingpledge.org/#eli+and+edythe+_broad.
13. http://givingpledge.org/#jeff_skoll.
14. http://givingpledge.org/#pierre+_omidyar.
15. Olivier Zunz, *Philanthropy in America: A History* (Princeton, NJ: Princeton University Press, 2012).
16. http://givingpledge.org/#carl_icahn.
17. Louis Menand, *The Metaphysical Club: A Story of Ideas in America* (New York: Farrar, Straus and Giroux, 2001), chapter 12.
18. Ellen Condliffe Lagemann, *The Politics of Knowledge: The Carnegie Corporation, Philanthropy and Public Policy* (Chicago: University of Chicago Press, 1992).
19. Andrew Carnegie, "Wealth," in *The Gospel of Wealth and Other Timely Essays* (New York: Century, 1901), 75.

20. See http://www.merriam-webster.com/dictionary/charity.

21. Robert T. Grimm Jr., ed., *Notable American Philanthropists* (Westport, CT: Greenwood, 2002), 100.

22. Related perspectives typically reflect Carnegie's position, as expressed in the so-called Gospel of Wealth, that philanthropy could create opportunities for those who are willing to work for them (Carnegie, "Wealth"; Appleby, *Relentless Revolution*, 203–204). At the same time, this philosophy was built on notions of the "deserving" and the "undeserving" poor, with Carnegie depicting the wealthy as trustees of the public good and arguing that charity enabled laziness and rewarded bad behavior.

23. http://givingpledge.org/#eli+and+edythe+_broad.

24. Jeffrey Sachs, "Sachs on Globalization," *The Economist*, 24 June 2000, 81–83.

25. Carl J. Schramm, "Law Outside the Market: The Social Utility of the Private Foundation," *Harvard Journal of Law and Public Policy* 30, no. 1 (Fall 2006): 356–407.

26. Parker, *George Peabody*, 209.

27. http://www.peabodyhistorical.org/gpeabody.htm.

28. Peter Frumkin, *Strategic Giving: The Art and Science of Philanthropy* (Chicago: University of Chicago Press, 2006).

29. "The History of Philanthropy in the United States," http://www.cof.org/Learn/content.cfm?ItemNumber=730.

30. Carnegie, "Wealth," 8–11, 19, 42, 54–55.

31. Ibid., 14–15.

32. Zunz, *Philanthropy in America*, 183.

33. Foundation Center, 2011, http://foundationcenter.org.

34. Laurence R. Veysey, *The Emergence of the American University* (Chicago: University of Chicago Press, 1965); Frederick Rudolph, *The American College and University: A History* (Athens: University of Georgia Press, 1990).

35. Jonathan R. Cole, *The Great American University: Its Rise to Preeminence, Its Indispensable National Role, Why It Must Be Protected* (New York: PublicAffairs, 2009), 35.

36. Menand, *The Metaphysical Club*, chapter 11.

37. http://www.ellisonfoundation.org/content/history.

38. http://www.msdf.org/impact/urban-education/.

39. http://en.wikipedia.org/wiki/Oprah_Winfrey.

40. http://www.kauffman.org/about-foundation/vision-mission-and-approach.aspx.

41. http://www.kauffman.org/about-foundation/our-founder-ewing-kauffman.aspx.

42. Ibid.

## Chapter 5
## Charity and Philanthropy

1. Max Weber, *The Protestant Ethic and the Spirit of Capitalism*, trans. Talcott Parsons (New York: Scribner, 1958), 60.

2. http://www.forbes.com/sites/luisakroll/2011/05/19/the-worlds-biggest-givers/.

3. "A Family's Billions, Artfully Sheltered," *New York Times*, 26 November 2011.

4. *New York Times*, 2 December 1998, A10; *Newsweek*, 30 August 1999, 50.

5. http://givingpledge.org/.

6. Andrew Carnegie, "Wealth," in *The Gospel of Wealth and Other Timely Essays* (New York: Century, 1901), 15.

7. http://givingpledge.org/#laura+and+john+_arnold.

8. http://givingpledge.org/#pierre+_omidyar.

9. http://givingpledge.org/#eli+and+edythe+_broad.

10. http://en.wikipedia.org/wiki/Herbert_Sandler.

11. http://givingpledge.org/#herb+and+marion+_sandler.

12. http://givingpledge.org/#gerry+and+marguerite+_lenfest.

13. http://givingpledge.org/#harold_hamm.

14. http://givingpledge.org/#george+b.+_kaiser.

15. Andrew Ross Sorkin, "The Mystery of Steve Jobs's Public Giving," *New York Times Dealbook*, 29 August 2011, http://dealbook.nytimes.com/2011/08/29/the-mystery-of-steve-jobss-public-giving/.

16. http://quotationsbook.com/quote/32811/.

17. David Hackett Fischer, *Albion's Seed: Four British Folkways in America* (New York: Oxford University Press, 1989), 7.

18. Ibid., 167.

19. Ibid., 174.

20. Abram English Brown, *Faneuil Hall and Faneuil Market, or Peter Faneuil and His Gift* (Boston: Lee and Shepard, 1900), 20–25.

21. Fischer, *Albion's Seed*, 209.

22. The other "folkway" was a flow of English-speaking people from the borders of North Britain and Northern Ireland to the

Appalachian backcountry, primarily during the half century from 1718 to 1775.

23. Barrington Moore, *Social Origins of Dictatorship and Democracy: Lord and Peasant in the Making of the Modern World* (Boston: Beacon, 1993), chapter 3.

24. Ibid.

25. Alexis de Tocqueville, *Democracy in America* (New York: Penguin, 2003), as cited in http://www.toqonline.com/archives/v2n4/TOQv2n4Martell.pdf.

26. Olivier Zunz, *Philanthropy in America: A History* (Princeton, NJ: Princeton University Press, 2012), chapter 2.

27. Everett Carll Ladd, *The Ladd Report* (New York: Free Press, 1999), cited in Robert D. Putnam, *Bowling Alone: The Collapse and Revival of American Community* (New York: Simon and Schuster, 2000), 117.

28. http://economix.blogs.nytimes.com/2011/10/18/which-americans-are-most-generous-and-to-whom/.

29. Frederick Rudolph, *The American College and University: A History* (Athens: University of Georgia Press, 1990).

30. Ibid.

31. Frank G. Dickinson, *The Changing Position of Philanthropy in the American Economy* (New York: National Bureau of Economic Research, 1970), 42.

32. "The Land of the Handout," *Newsweek*, 29 September 1997, 34–36.

33. Adam Smith, *The Theory of Moral Sentiments* (1759; Indianapolis: Liberty Classics, 1969), 47.

34. Adam Smith, *The Wealth of Nations* (1776; New York: Modern Library, 1937), 14.

35. Kenneth Boulding, "Notes on a Theory of Philanthropy," in *Philanthropy and Public Policy*, ed. Frank G. Dickinson (Boston: National Bureau of Economic Research, 1962), 57–58.

36. Herbert A. Simon, "Altruism and Economics," *American Economic Review* 83, no. 2 (1993): 158.

37. Ibid., 160.

38. Jane Allyn Piliavin and Hong-Wen Charng, "Altruism: A Review of Recent Theory and Research," *Annual Review of Sociology* 16 (1990): 27–65.

39. Boulding, "Notes on a Theory of Philanthropy," 61.

40. Ibid., 62.

## Chapter 6
## American-Style Capitalism

1. John Maynard Keynes, "Economic Possibilities for Our Grandchildren," in *Essays in Persuasion* (New York: W. W. Norton, 1963), 369.

2. John Kenneth Galbraith, *American Capitalism: The Concept of Countervailing Power* (1952; repr., New Brunswick, NJ: Transaction Press, 2008).

3. Richard Posner, *A Failure of Capitalism: The Crisis of '08 and the Descent into Depression* (Cambridge, MA: Harvard University Press, 2009).

4. William Baumol, Robert Litan, and Carl Schramm, *Good Capitalism, Bad Capitalism, and the Economics of Growth and Prosperity* (New Haven, CT: Yale University Press, 2007).

5. "Wall St. Profits Were a Mirage but Huge Bonuses Were Real," *New York Times*, 18 December 2008, 1.

6. "U.S. Sails on Tranquil Economic Seas," *Washington Post*, 2 December 1996, 1.

7. Charles Duhigg and Keith Bradsher, "How the U.S. Lost Out on iPhone Work," *New York Times*, 21 January 2012, http://www.nytimes.com/2012/01/22/business/apple-america-and-a-squeezed-middle-class.html?pagewanted=all.

8. http://www.federalreserve.gov/boarddocs/Speeches/2002/default.htm.

9. http:// trends.collegeboard.org/downloads/College_Pricing_2011.pdf.

10. Jennifer L. Hochschild, *What's Fair? American Beliefs about Distributive Justice* (Cambridge, MA: Harvard University Press, 1981), 278 (emphasis added). See surveys of American attitudes toward equal opportunity.

11. "Young Students Become the New Cause for Big Donors," *New York Times*, 21 August 2005.

12. For a deeper exploration of this argument, see Philip Auerswald and Zoltan J. Acs, "Defining Prosperity," *The American Interest*, May/June 2009, 4–13.

13. Robert J. Shiller, *Finance and the Good Society* (Princeton, NJ: Princeton University Press, 2012), chapter 18.

14. Joseph E. Stiglitz, *The Price of Inequality* (New York: W. W. Norton, 2012), 265.

15. Olivier Zunz, *Philanthropy in America: A History* (Princeton, NJ: Princeton University Press, 2012), chapter 6.

16. Robert J. Shiller, *Finance and the Good Society* (Princeton, NJ: Princeton University Press, 2012), 208.

17. The Center on Philanthropy at Indiana University, "Bank of America Study of High Net-Worth Philanthropy–Initial Report," October 2006, http://www.philanthropy.iupui.edu/research/BAC+Study+of +HNW+Philanthropy_102606.pdf.

18. Dennis McIlnay, "Four Moments in Time," *Foundation* 39, no. 5 (1998), http://www.foundationnews.org/CME/article.cfm?ID=1053.

## Chapter 7
## The Global Perspective

1. http://pinterest.com/acsphilanthropy/pins/.

2. Philip E. Auerswald, *The Coming Prosperity: How Entrepreneurs Are Transforming the Global Economy* (Oxford: Oxford University Press, 2012).

3. For a statement on the nature and logic of capitalism, see Robert Heilbroner, *The Nature and Logic of Capitalism* (New York: Harper and Row, 1985). Of course, it is precisely the institutional framework that differs from country to country and not necessarily the logic of the system. For a discussion of the different institutional frameworks, see Michael Porter, *Can Japan Compete?* (London: Macmillan, 2000); on Japan, see Wolfgang Streech and Kozo Yamamura, *The Origins of Non-Liberal Capitalism: Germany and Japan in Comparison* (Ithaca, NY: Cornell University Press, 2002); on France, see Jonah D. Levy, *Tocqueville's Revenge: State, Society, and Economics in Contemporary France* (Boston: Harvard University Press, 1999); and on Sweden, see Zoltan J. Acs and Charlie Karlsson, *Institutions, Entrepreneurship and Firm Growth: The Case of Sweden*, special issue of *Small Business Economics* (2002).

4. http://www.google.com/search?q=the+world+in+2050&hl=en &qscrl=1&nord=1&rlz=1T4PRFA_enUS429US431&prmd=imvnsb &tbm=isch&tbo=u&source=univ&sa=X&ei=XAWsT_aDFoiG6QH8x My3BA&sqi=2&ved=0CGoQsAQ&biw=1536&bih=745.

5. http://www.brainyquote.com/quotes/authors/a/alexis_de _tocqueville_3.html.

6. Gordon S. Wood, *The Idea of America: Reflections on the Birth of the United States* (New York: Penguin, 2011).

7. Seymour Martin Lipset, *American Exceptionalism: A Double-Edged Sword* (New York: W. W. Norton, 1996), 22.

8. http://www.Ft.Com/FT500, June 2011.

9. Yves Beigbeder, "A French Bill Gates–like Philanthropist?" trans. Zachary Hebert, *Le Monde*, 14 July 2010. http://watchingamerica.com /News/61556/a-french-bill-gates-like-philanthropist/.

10. Francis Fukuyama, "The End of History?" *The National Interest*, Summer 1989, 3–18.

11. Richard Florida, *The Rise of the Creative Class* (New York: Basic Books, 2002).

12. http://www.economist.com/node/21552589.

13. Joseph E. Stiglitz, *The Price of Inequality* (New York: W. W. Norton, 2012), 289.

14. Lawrence Summers, "How the Land of Opportunity Can Combat Inequality," *Financial Times*, 16 July 2012, 15.

15. Paul Gilding, *The Great Disruption: Why the Climate Crisis Will Bring on the End of Shopping and the Birth of a New World* (New York: Bloomsbury, 2011).

16. Peter Drucker, *Entrepreneurship and Innovation* (New York: Harpers, 1985), 7.

17. David Audretsch, *The Entrepreneurial Society* (Oxford: Oxford University Press, 2007), 192.

18. Carl J. Schramm, *The Entrepreneurial Imperative: How America's Economic Miracle Will Reshape the World (and Change Your Life)* (New York: CollinsBusiness, 2006), 177 (emphasis added).

19. http://www.forbes.com/sites/luisakroll/2011/05/19/ the-worlds-biggest-givers/.

20. Ibid.

21. http://philanthropy.com/blogs/philanthropytoday/ giving-pledge-draws-first-chinese-commitment/26764.

22. http://www.usatoday.com/tech/news/2009-03-02-un-digital _N.htm.

23. http://www.philanthrocapitalism.net/bonus-chapters/ second-golden-age/.

## Epilogue
## Changing the Tax Laws

1. Robert Frank, *Richistan: A Journey through the American Wealth Boom and the Lives of the New Rich* (New York: Three Rivers Press, 2007).

2. Robert H. Frank, "Darwin, the Market Whiz," *New York Times*, 18 September 2011, 8.

3. Milton Friedman, "The Spending Tax as a Wartime Fiscal Measure," *American Economic Review* 33, no.1 (1943): 50–62.

4. Rana Foroohar, "Warren Buffett Is on a Radical Track," *Time*, 23 January 2012, 38.

5. http://www.brainyquote.com/quotes/authors/a/alexis_de _tocqueville_3.html.

6. Quoted in Greg Mankiw, "The Passions of the Estate Tax," *Greg Mankiw's Blog: Random Observations for Students of Economics* (blog), 8 June 2006, http://gregmankiw.blogspot.com/2006/06 /passions-of-estate-tax.html.

7. Quoted in ibid.

8. Andrew Carnegie, "Wealth," in *The Gospel of Wealth and Other Timely Essays* (New York: Century, 1901).

# INDEX

Note: Page numbers followed by "f" indicate figures.